T0288389

Praise for *Lincoln and Citizenship*

"An attorney, law professor, immigration specialist, former associate editor of the Lincoln Legal Papers, and author of the best book on Lincoln's legal career, Mark E. Steiner is uniquely qualified to describe and analyze Lincoln's evolving views of citizenship. Because that subject has been inadequately treated by previous historians, this thoroughly researched, convincingly argued book is an especially welcome addition to the Lincoln literature."

—**Michael Burlingame**, editor of *Sixteenth President-in-Waiting: Abraham Lincoln and the Springfield Dispatches of Henry Villard, 1860–1861*

"In this well-written work, Steiner traces the development of Lincoln's racial policies from a moderate antislavery position to his final support for Black voting rights. Along the way he also covers Lincoln's thinking on other aspects of citizenship, including access to the federal courts, state racial codes, immigration, and gender. The author has made a major contribution to scholarship on the development of Lincoln's political thought."

—**Burrus M. Carnahan**, author of *Act of Justice: Lincoln's Emancipation Proclamation and the Law of War*

"Mark Steiner's book offers a comprehensive analysis of Lincoln's changing views on the meaning of American citizenship. *Lincoln and Citizenship* explores the changing relationship between citizenship and suffrage. Relying on Lincoln's words, this copiously researched study connects Lincoln's changing views on the meaning of citizenship to the developing views of Americans."

—**Charles M. Hubbard**, editor of *Lincoln, the Law, and Presidential Leadership*

EDITED BY RICHARD W. ETULAIN
AND SYLVIA FRANK RODRIGUE

MARK E. STEINER

Lincoln and Citizenship

Southern Illinois University Press
Carbondale

Southern Illinois University Press
www.siupress.com

Printed in the United States of America

24 23 22 21 4 3 2 1

The Concise Lincoln Library has been made possible in part through a generous donation by the Leland E. and LaRita R. Boren Trust.

Volumes in this series have been published with support from the Abraham Lincoln Bicentennial Foundation, dedicated to perpetuating and expanding Lincoln's vision for America and completing America's unfinished work.

Jacket illustration adapted from a painting by Wendy Allen

Library of Congress Cataloging-in-Publication Data
Names: Steiner, Mark E., 1955– author.
Title: Lincoln and citizenship / Mark E. Steiner.
Description: Carbondale, IL : Southern Illinois University Press, 2021. | Series: Concise Lincoln library | Includes bibliographical references and index.
Identifiers: LCCN 2020029107 (print) | LCCN 2020029108 (ebook) | ISBN 9780809338122 (cloth ; alk. paper) | ISBN 9780809338139 (ebook)
Subjects: LCSH: Lincoln, Abraham, 1809–1865—Political and social views. | Lincoln, Abraham, 1809–1865—Relations with African Americans. | Citizenship—United States—History—19th century. | African Americans—Civil rights—History—19th century. | United States—Politics and government—1849–1877.
Classification: LCC E457.2 .S825 2021 (print) | LCC E457.2 (ebook) | DDC 973.7092—dc23
LC record available at https://lccn.loc.gov/2020029107
LC ebook record available at https://lccn.loc.gov/2020029108

Printed on recycled paper ♻

This paper meets the requirements of ANSI/NISO Z39.48-1992 (Permanence of Paper). ∞

For Emma and Hannah

CONTENTS

LINCOLN AND CITIZENSHIP

INTRODUCTION: "MY FELLOW CITIZENS"

From Springfield to Washington

Over the course of his political career, Lincoln used "fellow citizens" as a salutation in speeches more than a hundred times,[1] from his 1832 "Communication to the People of Sangamo County" to a response to a serenade in the last week of his life. His use of the phrase may have been most pronounced during his eleven-day journey to Washington, DC, after he left Springfield as president-elect in February 1861. Along the way Lincoln addressed crowds gathered at train stations, state capitols, and hotels.[2] He would greet these crowds with different salutations, most often using "fellow citizens." In one speech in Pittsburgh, he used the phrase seven times in his brief talk.[3] It is not clear, though, what Lincoln meant when he addressed his fellow citizens. Who were they?

In one speech at the steps of the capitol in Columbus, Ohio—the only occasion in his journey to Washington when Lincoln used the word *citizenship*—he remarked, "Judging from what I see, I infer that that reception was one without party distinction, and one of entire kindness—one that had nothing in it beyond a feeling of the citizenship of the United States of America."[4] Lincoln was suggesting that the members of the assembly were joined together by a sense of community, a sense of national identity.

The salutation Lincoln used almost as often on his 1861 journey to Washington was "ladies and gentlemen." Did he see any difference between the two greetings? Were women also citizens? Lincoln made it clear that women had no serious role to play in the ongoing drama over secession through his acceptance of traditional gender roles. In his brief remarks to the crowd gathered at each stop, he invariably mentioned that many ladies were there to see him but that he had "decidedly the best of the bargain."[5] He told the crowd at Painesville, Ohio, that rarely had he seen "so many good-looking ladies" on one of his stops. Lincoln regretted not being able to give a speech in Newark, Ohio, because it deprived him of "addressing the many fair ladies assembled."[6]

In Cincinnati, Lincoln expressed pro-immigration views he had held as a Whig in the 1840s when he addressed a committee representing German workers. The chair of the committee spoke of workingmen as the basis of all governments, and Lincoln happily agreed with that sentiment: "not only of the native born citizens, but also of the Germans and foreigners from other countries," of whom he said, "I esteem them no better than other people, nor any worse." When he saw "a people borne down by the weight of their shackles," Lincoln added, he did not want to make their lives any worse. He wanted to do all he could "to raise the yoke." Since the United States was "extensive and new, and the countries of Europe are densely populated," Lincoln welcomed "any abroad who desire to make this the land of their adoption."[7]

In Philadelphia, Lincoln was the most philosophical. Filled with "deep emotion" at Independence Hall, the birthplace of the Declaration of Independence and the Constitution, Lincoln declared that all the political sentiments he held had "originated, and were given to the world from the hall in which we stand." Lincoln affirmed he never had "a feeling politically that did not spring from the sentiments embodied" in the Declaration. The Declaration of Independence was about more than separating from England; it gave "hope to the world for all future time." While Lincoln never expressly mentioned slavery in any speech on the trip, in Philadelphia he added an antislavery message when he noted the Declaration's "promise that in due time the weights should be lifted from the shoulders of all men, and that *all* should have an equal chance."[8] A reporter for the *New York Herald* wondered what Lincoln meant: "Does the President elect speak of 'men' in the aggregate as a nation or a community aspiring to nationality, or does he refer to man in his individual capacity—white, red, yellow or black?" Based on Lincoln's 1858 campaign speeches in his run for the US Senate, the reporter concluded that Lincoln "means the individual man" and that Lincoln's interpretation of the Declaration "puts the white and the black on the same footing of natural equality." Lincoln's notion that "the weights should be lifted from the shoulders of all men" meant "nothing more nor less than the progressive steps of African emancipation."[9]

Although Lincoln called for all men to have an equal chance, he did not mean all men should have equal rights and be citizens. The New York reporter astutely observed that Lincoln believed white and black people should be "on the same footing of natural equality." Lincoln attacked slavery because it denied the natural rights of black people; he did not yet believe, however, that black people were entitled to the equal rights of citizenship.

The Meanings of Citizenship

Citizenship was a developing concept in antebellum America.[10] In 1862 Edward Bates, Lincoln's attorney general, lamented the lack of a "clear and satisfactory definition of the phrase *citizen of the United States.*"[11] During Lincoln's lifetime, citizenship was sometimes seen as reciprocal duties of allegiance and protection. Military service would loom large as an obligation of citizenship. Citizenship also was tied to rights; this is how most Americans today view citizenship—as the "right to have rights."[12] But Lincoln and many of his contemporaries divided rights into distinct categories. The most basic rights were natural rights, the right to "life, liberty, and the pursuit of happiness." Lincoln consistently said black people were entitled to their natural rights. Civil rights consisted of legal entitlements "essential to pursuing a livelihood and protecting one's personal security"; they included such rights as owning property and going to court. Political rights included voting and holding office. Voting was becoming emblematic of citizenship, but some states, including Illinois, allowed noncitizens to vote.[13]

At its most basic level, though, citizenship is about membership in a political community. The crucial questions Lincoln and others asked were these: Who belongs to and who does not belong to this political community?

This book explores what citizenship meant to Lincoln at different times in his political career. For most of his career, it was clear to him that white males were members of this community. Women and racialized others were not.[14]

* * *

In the first chapter, I examine Lincoln's 1836 call for "admitting all whites to the right of suffrage, who pay taxes or bear arms, (by no means excluding females)."[15] This was a peculiar statement. For one thing, by limiting suffrage to taxpayers and militia members, Lincoln was calling for a rollback from universal white male suffrage, which had existed in Illinois since it became a state in 1818. For another, allowing taxpayers to vote would have given some women voting rights, which Lincoln expressly recognized. When Lincoln entered politics, women were not members of any political community in the United States. Lincoln may have been carried away by an odd combination of Whig conservatism and a legalistic formalism he had imbued from the legal treatises he was reading as he prepared for the bar. Suffrage was an issue in 1836—and 1840—because Whigs wanted to capitalize on Martin Van Buren's support for limited black suffrage at the 1821 New York Constitutional Convention.

I examine Lincoln's disdain for nativism in the second chapter. In the 1840s and 1850s, Lincoln addressed another aspect of citizenship—whether immigrants belonged to the political community. Nativists in the 1840s and 1850s questioned whether recent immigrants were part of the American polity and recommended longer waiting periods for naturalization and for suffrage. Lincoln believed all male European immigrants belonged to this community; he thought the Declaration of Independence provided basic values that defined what it meant to be an American, which unified all those who believed in those ideals. Since citizenship was essentially creedal, Lincoln rejected the anti-immigrant nativism common in the antebellum North.

In the 1840s, Lincoln joined with other Whigs in restricting voting rights to citizens. It was a move contrary to the 1818 Illinois Constitution, which did not link voting to citizenship—a noncitizen had to reside in the state for only six months before being able to vote. Alien suffrage, for a time, somehow coexisted with the notion that voting was the most important attribute of citizenship. The Whig platform followed the idea put forth in the 1839 *Law Dictionary*, in which John Bouvier, a naturalized citizen, defined *citizen* as "one who, under the constitution and laws of the United States, has a right to vote for representatives in congress and other public officers, and who is qualified to fill offices in the gift of the people."[16]

In chapter 3, I discuss Lincoln's support for Illinois's Black Laws and for colonization. Lincoln, for most of his adult life, could not imagine African Americans belonging to the political community of the United States. He supported the Black Laws of Illinois that prohibited blacks from voting, serving on juries, or testifying in court against a white man. Lincoln never wavered in his support. His understanding of the Declaration of Independence led him to antislavery convictions, but those antislavery convictions only went so far. In Illinois, Lincoln was not an abolitionist. Rejecting both slavery and black citizenship, Lincoln chose what was then considered the "moderate" path of colonization. Black citizenship and colonization were antithetical. Black citizenship would mean that black people belonged to the political community; colonization meant that blacks did not even belong in the United States.

The most notorious antebellum discussion of black citizenship was Chief Justice Roger Taney's opinion in *Dred Scott.* Taney wrote that black people could not be citizens of the United States because they were "beings of an inferior order" with "no rights which the white man was bound to respect." Lincoln's responses to *Dred Scott* are the subject of chapter 4. His initial reaction was an answer to Stephen Douglas's speech on the case, in which Douglas presented a nightmare scenario of racial equality that had been averted by the Supreme Court. Lincoln, like Douglas, focused his attention on Taney's holding on citizenship. Lincoln argued that Taney was wrong about the history of black citizenship during the founding era. Lincoln's emphasis on the citizenship holding was unusual for a politician who did not support black citizenship. It is likely that, as a lawyer, Lincoln could not help himself, as that part of Taney's opinion was particularly weak.

In 1858 Lincoln ran against Douglas for a seat in the US Senate. Douglas predictably attacked Lincoln and his fellow Republicans for their support of black citizenship. Lincoln did not continue his earlier attack on Taney's holding on citizenship. Instead he reaffirmed his opposition to black citizenship. Douglas continued to press Lincoln on this point, and Lincoln continued to disclaim any support for "making voters or jurors out of negroes."[17] Lincoln did consistently argue that blacks were entitled to natural rights. His stances on blacks having natural rights but not citizenship rights were the mainstream Republican views before the Civil War.

In the last chapter, I argue that Lincoln supported large-scale colonization schemes for the first two years of his presidency. Lincoln publicly advocated for colonization in his annual messages to Congress in 1861 and 1862 and in his lecture to a "deputation of Negroes" in August 1862.[18] But after a fruitless scheme for resettling blacks in Chiriquí in Central America and an ill-fated project in Haiti, Lincoln gave up on large-scale colonization. He never publicly mentioned colonization after his annual message in December 1862. I further argue that Lincoln slowly warmed to the idea of black citizenship. He changed his mind about black men's capacity for citizenship because of the record of black troops in the Civil War. Lincoln initially had resisted the enlistment of black troops, not only because of political considerations, but because he thought black men lacked manly virtues such as bravery. He was disabused of that notion, however. He also was encouraged by his meetings at the White House with Frederick Douglass and other black leaders. In his last public address, Lincoln discussed black suffrage in Louisiana and suggested that the "elective franchise" be "conferred on the very intelligent, and on those who serve our cause as soldiers."[19]

A Note on the N-Word

In this book, I quote Lincoln and others using the N-word. Sadly, that seems unavoidable in a book about Abraham Lincoln and citizenship.[20] In the course of my research, the word showed up a lot, mostly in issues of the *Sangamo Journal* during the elections of 1836 and 1840, when Lincoln and other Whigs used race-baiting attacks against Martin Van Buren; during the Senate campaign of 1858, when both Lincoln and Douglas used the word in campaign speeches and Democrats and Republicans freely used the term "nigger equality"; and during the Civil War, when white northerners debated the use of black troops and emancipation. I have tried to be careful about the word's use. Its appearances are not gratuitous.

The use of the N-word by white Americans during Lincoln's time was racist. Scholars agree that the word "was a seminal anti-black term that gained virulence as a slur in the 1820s and 1830s."[21] In 1829 David Walker observed that "white Americans have applied this term to Africans, by way of reproach for our colour, to aggravate and heighten our miseries, because they have their feet on our throats."[22] Hosea Easton, in 1837, explained that the word was an opprobrious term "employed to impose contempt upon them as an inferior race, and also to express their deformity of person."[23] Historian Elizabeth Stordeur Pryor notes that whites' use of the epithet inscribed "black people as un-American"; whites used the epithet "to pose black citizenship as unimaginable."[24]

CHAPTER ONE

WHEN LINCOLN WHIGGED OUT ON SUFFRAGE

Abraham Lincoln's first pronouncement on citizenship came during the 1836 election campaign. It was an anachronistic and perplexing statement that called for both limiting and expanding suffrage.

In the June 11, 1836, edition of the *Sangamo Journal*, the Whig newspaper in Springfield, a letter signed by "Many Voters" appeared. Recognizing that the names of candidates were starting to appear in the paper in advance of the August state elections (the presidential election would be held in November), the letter writers stated that "the times demand from them [the candidates] a declaration of their political doctrines at as early a period as possible." Only then would the people "be better prepared to judge of their qualifications and fitness to serve them."[1]

Lincoln answered the call "at as early a period as possible"—the next issue of the *Sangamo Journal*. He described the letter as calling upon candidates "to show their hands" and replied, "Agreed. Here's mine." Lincoln began with his position on suffrage: "I go for all sharing the privileges of the government, who assist in bearing its burthens. Consequently I go for admitting all whites to the right of suffrage, who pay taxes or bear arms, (by no means excluding females.)"[2] These two sentences have drawn some attention from Lincoln scholars, particularly the parenthetical part, but there has not been any sustained analysis of the meaning of Lincoln's statement.

Van Buren, Voting Rights, and the 1836 Election

Suffrage had become an issue worth addressing because Whigs were attacking Martin Van Buren, the Democratic candidate for president, for his statement of support for limited black suffrage at the 1821 New York Constitutional Convention. Lincoln's position on suffrage, which limited voting to taxpayers and militia members, was more restrictive than the 1818 Illinois Constitution, which mandated universal white male suffrage. Lincoln somehow rejected both the Illinois constitutional provision for suffrage and the Jacksonian trend toward universal white male suffrage. He apparently accepted, however, Illinois's stance on alien suffrage: the 1818 Constitution allowed noncitizens to vote if they resided in Illinois; it did not require them to wait until they were naturalized.[3] Lincoln was not calling for women's suffrage; he was advocating that voting be restricted to those who fulfilled civic obligations such as paying taxes, which could include some women. This position was not looking toward a future of "woman rights"; it was looking, rather, toward an old idea of suffrage based on civic contributions.

Why did Lincoln choose to address suffrage in a relatively brief announcement? Some historians have suggested that suffrage was an issue in 1836 because a large number of Irish laborers were working on the Illinois and Michigan Canal.[4] But the "foreign" vote was not yet a controversial issue in Springfield.[5] While work on the canal had begun in 1836, it did not start until summer and not much progress was made that summer and autumn.[6] After the state election in August and the presidential election in November, the *Sangamo Journal* did not complain about the Irish vote.[7] The controversy over Irish canal workers began in the next cycle of elections in 1838, when Whigs claimed that these itinerate workers had voted fraudulently by not establishing residency.[8] Whigs complained that elections were being decided by immigrant railroad and canal workers.[9] Some Whigs began questioning whether the practice of allowing noncitizens to vote should continue.[10] These complaints did not come just from high-minded notions about the purity of elections; Whigs were angry about election results. In 1839 the *Sangamo Journal* began grumbling about "foreign office-holders," noting that the sheriff of Cook County had been reelected despite not being a citizen.[11]

But, in 1836, complaints about the Irish canal workers were inconsequential. The only reason why suffrage was an issue in Illinois that summer owed to the presidential race. Whigs were relying heavily on race-baiting to attack Martin Van Buren, the Democratic presidential candidate, and Richard Mentor Johnson, his running mate.[12] Whigs attacked Van Buren for favoring black suffrage in New York and vilified Johnson for having children with a black woman.[13] Whigs also attacked Van Buren for not supporting universal white male suffrage at the New York Constitutional Convention.[14]

The Illinois Whig press constantly attacked Van Buren for supporting "free Negro suffrage." The attack was so pervasive that some articles assumed the reader would understand even veiled references to Van Buren. For example, a November 1835 article—a full year before the presidential election—warned that Illinois "is threatened to be overrun with free negroes." The article concluded, "We do not want the negroes who will be thus thrown upon us: they should be sent to *N. York!*" That would be, of course, Van Buren's New York.[15]

Most articles were not so subtle. The *Sangamo Journal* explained how Van Buren held "free Negro doctrines," which led him at the New York Constitutional Convention to introduce an "article into the Constitution of that state, placing the *free negro and the white man on equal grounds at the ballot box!*"[16] In another article, the *Journal* opined that "the most superficial observer" could understand Van Buren's motivation for "extending the right of suffrage to free negroes." Since Van Buren knew "the incapacity of the negroes, (that unfortunate and degraded race)," he must have supported black suffrage because he needed voters who lacked virtue and intelligence.[17] Another article gave a brief summary: "Martin is in favor of admitting opulent negroes to, and excluding poor whites from, the right of suffrage."[18] For further race-baiting purposes, the *Journal* would call the supporters of Hugh White the "White Party" and claim these supporters "know that Mr. Van Buren is in favor of extending the right of suffrage to negroes."[19]

The *Sangamo Journal* also printed a letter written in imitation of black dialect. Lincoln biographer Michael Burlingame believes Lincoln was the letter's likely author.[20] Lincoln often contributed anonymous or pseudonymous pieces to the *Journal*.[21] William H. Herndon, Lincoln's law partner and biographer, noted that newspaper editor Simeon Francis was "warmly attached to Lincoln" and entertained great admiration for his "brains and noble qualities." Herndon believed that Lincoln exercised undisputed control of the columns of the *Journal* itself: "Whatever he wrote or had written, went into the editorial pages without question."[22]

The letter's point was to explain why black men would vote for Van Buren (Wanjuren, in the letter's dialect) and Johnson:

> Massa Prenter:
> When I was up dare in Spriegfield the pepul kep axin me, How's the election gwine down in your parts? Now I couldnt den exactly precisely tell how de folks was gwine—but I been asken all around sence, and I gest wants to tell presactly how it is. De gemm'en ob color all gwine for dat man wat writes de epitaphs of truth and vartue wid a syringe—some to Mr. Katshoun, and skuire the Builder. Dis brings me to a write understandin—for to no what makes de niggers all vote for dese men.
>
> Now I spose you knows as how you sees dese men goes for Wanjuren, and that dare tudder man wat lub de nigger so. Wanjuren says de nigger all shall vote, and dat oder man in Kentucky state, is goin to make all the nigger women's children white. Oh hush, ha, he. ho! Youd split your sides laffin to hear Capun—tell how much Wanjuren is going to do for de nigger—de ways deys goin for him, man—oh, hush! and dat man who used to buse old Jackson so, case as how he was ginst the niggers votin—ah, law! de way he roots for Wanjuren now is sorter singular—he look precisely like a pig off in a Coln Field—wid one ear marked, so he massa know

> 'em. De way de niggers is going for him now. oh hush! And skuire, the builder, de ways dey is going to run him ahead em all aint nobodys business—kase as how hese goin to send all dese poore white folks off to Library, and let the free niggers vote—and wen we send all dese tarnal white folks off, we'se goin to send him to Kongress, and den de niggers will be in town! oh, hush!
>
> In grait haist, yours, SEES.HER.[23]

Lincoln's letter—and its abundant use of the N-word—fits perfectly within the category of what Elizabeth Stordeur Pryor calls "blackface literary productions" in America. White humorists would put the N-word in the mouths of black caricatures as "a smoking gun of African American backwardness, one that took direct aim at black people who moved through public space."[24] Lincoln, like other white purveyors of blackface, was using black dialect to highlight differences and to oppose black citizenship.

This attack on Van Buren for supporting "free Negro" suffrage had surfaced earlier that year in the Illinois House of Representatives. After the state senate endorsed Hugh White over Van Buren, the Democrats in the Illinois House passed their own resolutions on the upcoming presidential race. One resolution expressed "the most perfect confidence in the patriotism, integrity, and Democratic Republic principles" of Martin Van Buren and his running mate, Richard Mentor Johnson. These resolutions passed thirty-one to twenty. Lincoln voted no with his fellow Whigs.[25]

Although heavily outnumbered, the Whigs in the House did not go down without a fight. Led by Lincoln and Edwin B. Webb, the Whigs executed a series of parliamentary maneuvers: moving to amend, amending the amendment, and dividing the question. They also introduced amendments to the pro–Van Buren resolutions designed to trap Democrats into opposing either universal white male suffrage or the (fifteen-year-old) views of their presidential candidate: "*RESOLVED*, That all white male citizens of the age of 21 years and upwards, are entitled to the privilege of voting whether they hold real estate or not. *RESOLVED*, That the elective franchise should be kept pure from contamination by the admission of colored votes."[26] The amendments constituted counter-propositions to the positions held by Van Buren at the New York Constitutional Convention.

All but one of the twenty Whig legislators who voted against the Van Buren resolutions now voted for the amendments in favor of universal white male suffrage and against black suffrage. Lincoln voted in favor of universal white male suffrage and against black suffrage. The Whigs were joined by sixteen of the legislators who had voted for the Van Buren resolutions. Fifteen of the Democratic legislators who had voted in favor of the Van Buren resolutions now voted against universal white male suffrage and in favor of black suffrage. The onslaught of parliamentary maneuvers may have resulted in those legislators reflexively voting against whatever the Whigs proposed. It is also possible that they saw the amendments as an attack on Van Buren and thought it wise to support their candidate.[27] In any event, the *Sangamo Journal* had great fun claiming that the Democrats were against universal white male suffrage and in favor of black suffrage.[28] These votes by Democrats in the Illinois House, claimed the *Journal*, "were in perfect accordance with the opinions of Mr. Van Buren, as declared in the New York state Convention."[29]

While New York's 1777 Constitution had established a property requirement for suffrage, it was not racially restrictive: any male who owned a freehold could vote, depending on how much his freehold was worth and which elective office was involved (voting for senators required a larger freehold than voting for representatives).[30] The initial recommendation on suffrage at the 1821 New York Constitutional Convention restricted voting to "white male citizens" but broadened the qualifications to include anyone who paid taxes or worked on a public road or was enrolled in the militia. Reporters at the convention accurately stated that "a long desultory debate ensued." Proponents of the change argued those "who contribute to the public support, we consider as entitled to a share in the election of rulers." A few delegates such as conservative jurist James Kent were opposed to any change in the property requirement; Kent refused to "bow before the idol of universal suffrage." Others, like Van Buren, thought the proposed change went too far, believing that "many evils would flow from a wholly unrestricted suffrage." The initial recommendation pertaining to white men passed; however, the complete exclusion of black men from suffrage was rejected. The delegates agreed to allow blacks to continue to vote if they met a property requirement of $250. Van Buren argued in favor of this requirement from the 1777 New York Constitution, contending that it would be unfair to tax blacks who held property and then not allow them to vote. The property requirement itself would be "but inducements to industry."[31] Very few blacks met this requirement; in 1825, only 298 blacks out of 29,701 qualified to vote.[32] Van Buren's statements and votes were not controversial at the time. But, in 1836, when universal white male suffrage was widespread, these stances were now unpopular.

Vice presidential candidate Richard Mentor Johnson was also the subject of Whig attacks. He did not hide his relationship with his slave Julia Chinn and treated their two daughters as his own. The *Journal* clipped this short notice from the *Alton Telegraph*: "The *Illinois Republican* says 'Richard M. Johnson disapproved of all distinctions in society, but from personal merit.' It seems so—no better proof wanted, than taking a black woman to his bed and board."[33] The *Journal* also claimed that Johnson did not object to black suffrage because he would not "adopt any principles in regard to the right of suffrage that would disfranchise his family connexions."[34] Twenty-two years later, Lincoln was still referring to Johnson's "amalgamation" during the Senate race with Douglas.[35]

Van Buren, Voting Rights, and the 1840 Election

Lincoln and other Whigs continued these attacks in the 1840 election, when Van Buren ran for reelection against William Henry Harrison; they again wanted to use Van Buren's participation in the New York Constitutional Convention of 1821 against him.[36] Lincoln instructed fellow Whig Richard F. Barrett, who was traveling in New York, to obtain the books necessary for Whig attacks: "Do not fail to procure a copy of the *Journal* of the New York Convention of 1821. I sometimes see the *Debates* of the New York Convention refered to, and I am not sure whether the *Journal* & *Debates* are one & the same, or distinct. If they are distinct, try to procure both. I would not miss your getting them for a hundred dollars."[37] Lincoln authorizing spending $100 for these books meant that he was willing to pay a heavy premium to document Van Buren's support of black suffrage.

The Whigs in 1840 largely repackaged their 1836 criticism of Van Buren's stances at the 1821 convention (Johnson was dropped from the Democratic ticket).[38] In a speech at Tremont, Illinois, in May 1840, Lincoln "reviewed the political course of Mr. Van Buren, and especially his votes in the New York convention in allowing Free Negroes the right of suffrage."[39] In a debate with Stephen Douglas, Lincoln asserted that Van Buren "had voted for Negro suffrage under certain limitations." After Douglas denied this was true, Lincoln read from Holland's *Life of Van Buren.* Douglas claimed it was a forgery, and Lincoln quoted a letter from Van Buren stating the book was accurate. James H. Matheny reported, "Douglas got mad—Snatched up the book and Slung it into the crowd—saying d—n such a book."[40] This was the last time Lincoln outplayed Douglas in raising the specter of black citizenship.

The Whigs made one new argument by criticizing Van Buren for allowing black witnesses to testify against a white officer in a court-martial. The *Sangamo Journal* ran three articles about the topic in July 1840 alone. One article was headlined "More Love for Free Negroes!"; another, "A Most Extraordinary Act of Mr. Van Buren. Negro Servants allowed by him to testify in Court against White Men."[41]

While it is not clear whether these attacks by Whigs worked any better than they had in 1836, Van Buren lost.

Lincoln's Rollback of Suffrage

From the American Revolution to the Civil War, voting rights initially depended on owning property, then on fulfilling a service or obligation to the state, and finally on being white and male. Because the US Constitution did not prescribe qualifications for the right to vote, determining who was eligible to vote was left up to the individual states. After 1776 most of the newly formed states retained some sort of property requirement. Over the next fifty years, the original thirteen states roughly moved from a freehold requirement, to an intermediate phase that allowed taxpayers or militia members to vote, and on to the final stage of universal white male suffrage.[42] The requirements of owning property or paying taxes that were nearly universal at the time of the American Revolution were in retreat by 1818. By 1824 twenty-one out of twenty-four states had universal white male suffrage.[43]

The State of Illinois adopted universal white male suffrage. Its 1818 Constitution granted suffrage on the basis of age, gender, race, and residence: "all white male inhabitants above the age of twenty-one years, having resided in the State six months next preceding the election" had the right to vote.[44] Municipalities were able to set their own suffrage qualifications for local elections. While state elections favored universal white male suffrage, municipalities sometimes kept taxpayer or property qualifications. When Chicago was incorporated as a city in 1837, its electorate was limited to taxpayers.[45] When Springfield incorporated in 1840, it granted suffrage to "all free white male inhabitants, citizens of the United States."[46]

Lincoln's call for limiting suffrage to "all whites" who "pay taxes or bear arms" was decidedly out of step. He was rejecting the egalitarianism of the day and the universal white male suffrage enshrined in the 1818 Illinois Constitution. He certainly was not echoing his fellow Illinois Whigs; Whig candidates who had published similar letters that summer in the *Sangamo Journal* supported universal white male suffrage. For example, Andrew M'Cormick made it clear that he was against suffrage for free black men, against any property qualifications, and for "the doctrine that every white citizen of lawful age shall possess the right of electing or being elected to office."[47] R. L. Wilson stated that he "must unqualifiedly hold that all white male inhabitants possessing a constitutional qualification whether opulent or indigent" should have the right of suffrage.[48] Ninian Edwards rejected any property qualifications, as the right of voting "should not depend upon the weight of the voter's purse." Edwards also claimed that any opinion in favor of giving blacks the vote resulted from ignorance or lack of principle.[49]

During the 1836 presidential campaign, Illinois Whigs excoriated Van Buren for his failure to support universal white male suffrage back in 1821; fifteen years later, Lincoln the Whig failed to support universal white male suffrage. He even contradicted his own vote in favor of universal white male suffrage cast earlier that year in the Illinois legislature. Lincoln was echoing Thomas Jefferson's "fights or pays" qualification for suffrage; in an 1816 letter Jefferson had called for "general suffrage": "Let every man who fights or pays, exercise his just and equal right in their election." But Jefferson had been reacting to Virginia's fifty-acre freehold requirement for suffrage and was arguing for an expansion of voting rights.[50] Whether Lincoln was aware of Jefferson's stance on suffrage, he was nevertheless advocating a position that historian Bruce Levine has accurately described as "vestigial elitism."[51] Other Whigs had already accepted white male suffrage because they realized that battle was lost and they still had elections to win.[52] A few months before Lincoln stated his views on suffrage, a writer in the conservative *American Quarterly Review* wrote, "The day is past for arguing the question of universal suffrage on this side of the Atlantic."[53] By 1828 universal white male suffrage was entrenched.[54] Lincoln was proposing a rollback.

Military Service and Citizenship

Lincoln's basing suffrage upon militia service may have come from a cultural connection between citizenship and military service or may have reflected his recent experience as a volunteer in the Black Hawk War.[55] After signing a treaty requiring the Sac and Fox tribes to remain west of the Mississippi River, Black Hawk, a Sac chief, led 800 Sacs and Foxes into Illinois to plant their spring crops on their traditional lands. This action led to a hysterical overreaction by white settlers as Black Hawk was pursued by the 340 troops of regular army under the command of General Henry Atkinson and 1,700 Illinois militia members.

Lincoln was among the militiamen who volunteered from Sangamon County. Although all white males between the ages of eighteen and forty-five were enrolled in the militia, members volunteered in times of war. Lincoln volunteered for a thirty-day enlistment. Each militia unit elected its own officers, and Lincoln was elected captain. Lincoln reenlisted twice and served a total of eighty days. Less than one-quarter of the eligible men in Sangamon County volunteered, and only 1.3 percent of the eligible men served in three or more units.[56] Lincoln succinctly described the experience: he joined "the campaign, served near three months, met the ordinary hardships of such an expedition, but was in no battle."[57]

Lincoln was proud of his service and thought it was important. He always mentioned it whenever he was asked to provide his biography.[58] In a "little sketch" he sent Jesse W. Fell in 1859, he mentioned that being elected captain was "a success which gave me more pleasure than any I have had since."[59] After the *Sangamo Journal* inadvertently omitted Lincoln's name from a list of political candidates who had served in the Black Hawk War, it published a correction noting that "Capt. Lincoln" was one of those "who were on the frontiers periling their lives in the service of their country."[60] It seems likely that Captain Lincoln was the one who had pointed out the omission.

Lincoln did not explicitly criticize the Illinois constitutional provision that allowed noncitizens to vote. Because voting was not yet tied to citizenship and because states could prescribe voting requirements, some states, such as Illinois, allowed alien suffrage.[61] The Illinois Constitution allowed "inhabitants" to vote; citizenship was not required. As citizenship was becoming inextricably linked with voting, some Whigs were beginning to criticize alien suffrage. (In the Northeast, nativist Whigs had a problem with immigrants voting at all.) Lincoln, whether purposely or not, avoided this issue by including neither *inhabitant* nor *citizen* in his statement on suffrage. He would later attack alien suffrage.

"By No Means Excluding Females"

Though women did not serve in the militia, unmarried women with property would have paid taxes. The Illinois statute on revenue plainly stated that the sheriff for each county would proceed to collect taxes "by calling upon each owner of the same, at *his or her* place of residence."[62] Seven percent of landowners on the county tax lists in the mid-1830s in Sugar Creek in Sangamon County were women.[63] Under the legal doctrine of coverture, married women did not have a legal identity, and their husbands owned their property.[64] Therefore, any women who owned property were unmarried or widowed.[65]

Lincoln certainly would have read about coverture in Blackstone's *Commentaries on the Laws of England*.[66] Blackstone explained how "by marriage, the husband and wife are one person in law: that is, the very being or legal existence of the woman is suspended during the marriage, or at least incorporated and consolidated into that of the husband."[67] Lincoln's taxpaying requirement meant that only women who were *femmes soles* (unmarried or widowed women) would be able to vote, not married women, who, as *femmes couvertes*, would not have owned any property that was taxable. Such a restriction would have limited suffrage to a few wealthier women at certain stages of their lives—before marriage or after their husband's death.[68] And it would have kept coverture intact, as married women still would have remained legally invisible.

It is tempting to read much into Lincoln's parenthetical comment, "by no means excluding females," but it does not represent any prescient support for voting rights for women. William H. Herndon may have been the first to misinterpret Lincoln's remarks on suffrage. In letters written fifty years later, Herndon viewed those 1836 remarks in the context of the women's rights movement that came later. Herndon said Lincoln "declared himself for woman's rights" in 1836 as "his keen sense of justice could not refuse woman the rights which he demanded for himself."[69] "Seeing that woman was denied in free America her right to the elective franchise," Herndon wrote, Lincoln "always advocated her rights." But Herndon also conceded that Lincoln thought "the time probably had not yet come to openly advocate the idea before the people." Herndon did not explain why Lincoln was willing to advocate openly for women's suffrage in 1836 but not later. Herndon recalled Lincoln telling him, "This question is one simply of time."[70] In the late 1850s, Lincoln may have told a young suffragist that he believed she would vote "before you are much older than I."[71] As it turned out, though, she would have been much older than Lincoln when she finally got to vote, assuming she lived for another sixty years.

Political equality for women was not in the air in central Illinois in 1836. Neither women's rights nor women's suffrage is mentioned in Illinois newspapers until 1848. The earliest that one of the literary and debating societies in central Illinois discussed woman's suffrage was 1838. Lincoln participated in the New Salem Literary and Debating Society while living in New Salem, but there is no evidence that the group debated women's suffrage while Lincoln was there. In Farmer's Point, a few miles south of New Salem, the Tyro Polemic and Literary Club may have debated the question "Shall women have the right to vote?" but not until 1838.[72] The lyceums of Springfield apparently did not address women's suffrage either.[73] Notices for the Sangamon County Lyceum and Young Man's Lyceum regularly appeared in the *Sangamo Journal* in the 1830s. The lyceums featured such topics as colonization, common schools, matrimony, phrenology, capital punishment, dueling, and the banking system.[74] Neither women's suffrage nor women's rights was announced as a topic for either lyceum in the 1830s.

Lincoln was not calling for universal white suffrage for both men and women. He was not calling for political equality for white women. In 1836 such calls would have been nonexistent from any man running for any public office. The only male public figures who supported women's rights before the Civil War were abolitionists like Frederick Douglass and Wendell Phillips.[75]

There was some discussion of woman suffrage at this time. For example, in 1836, a review of British philosopher Samuel Bailey's *The Rationale of Political Representation* appeared in the conservative *American Quarterly Review.* The anonymous reviewer noted that Bailey called for "the right of women to participate in the elective franchise." Such a proposal challenged the separate spheres of men and women. The reviewer wholly questioned "the expediency of offering any portion of the female sex the smallest inducement to forget the private offices and domestic duties of life, or to become parties to political strife."[76]

The idea of suffrage for women was the most extreme plank of nineteenth-century feminism, but it was so outside the norm that for many it was unimaginable. The demand for suffrage was radical because it did not accept women's oppression in the private sphere but instead demanded "admission to citizenship, and through it admission to the public sphere," as historian Ellen Du Bois wrote.[77] But the idea of women as full citizens was inconceivable in antebellum America.[78]

The radicalism of women's suffrage can best be shown by events at the women's rights convention at Seneca Falls in 1848. Lucretia Mott had advised against including the suffrage resolution because it would make the proceedings "look ridiculous." Henry Stanton opposed the suffrage provision because it would turn the convention into a farce; he left town to avoid embarrassment. Elizabeth Cady Stanton and Susan B. Anthony later observed that "the only resolution that was not unanimously adopted was the ninth," which called for women to secure for themselves "their sacred right to the elective franchise." Stanton and Anthony noted, "Those who took part in the debate feared a demand for the right to vote would defeat others they deemed more rational, and make the whole movement ridiculous."[79] Facing opposition, the suffrage resolution was saved by Frederick Douglass, who argued that there could be "no reason in the world for denying to women the exercise of the elective franchise."[80]

Lincoln was not brazenly advocating women's suffrage twelve years before it was put forth at Seneca Falls. He was advocating that taxpayer suffrage be extended to include women who owned property—the logical consequence of suffrage based on taxation. It was the rational conclusion of the Revolutionary-era proposition of "no taxation without representation." A taxpaying or property-holding requirement for suffrage became a quandary in a patriarchal society. If anyone owning property was allowed to vote, and a woman owns property, then the conclusion that she should be allowed to vote was perfectly logical, if totally unacceptable.

That taxpaying women would be allowed to vote was a common argument against suffrage based on taxpaying. The conservative writer Samuel Jones in his 1842 treatise on suffrage argued that "mere performance" of common duties like paying taxes or serving in the militia should not entitle anyone to vote. (Jones still believed in property requirements.) He noted, "Females, minors, and foreigners not naturalized are liable to be taxed and do actually pay taxes; and if that, of itself, gives the right of suffrage, they ought to be admitted to the exercise of that right; otherwise they are taxed wrongfully. But they are every where excluded; and the advocates of the doctrine have always acquiesced in their exclusion."[81] The argument that a taxpaying requirement would allow women to vote was also made at antebellum constitutional conventions.[82]

The concept of women's rights was certainly in the air after 1848. The *Sangamo Journal*, in August 1848, remarked that the "woman's convention" was assembled at Seneca Falls to discuss women's "social, civil, and religious conditions and rights."[83] Afterward, stories about women's rights conventions were regularly published in Illinois newspapers. For example, in 1850, the *Journal* sarcastically reported on a convention in Worcester, New York, where the equality of women was endorsed: "the right to vote, to hold office, and go to battle, if necessary, leaving men to take their share of the kitchen, nursery, etc."[84] But Lincoln never again broached the subject.

Lincoln's advocacy of limited suffrage for women was, in its own way, anachronistic in 1836. The last state that had allowed women to vote was New Jersey, which ended the practice in 1807. New Jersey had permitted woman who met a property requirement to vote. In New Salem, a steady diet of legal-treatise formalism and Enlightenment rationalism led Lincoln to the "pure republican logic" of women taxpayers voting.[85]

How did Lincoln come to hold the views on suffrage he espoused in the *Sangamo Journal* in 1836? In New Salem, Lincoln read Enlightenment writers like Thomas Paine, Edward Gibbon, and Constantin de Volney.[86] The influence of these writers can be overstated. Robert Bray suggests that Lincoln's reading of Volney made him a "radical democrat and a radical anticleric, at least for the next few years"; however, Lincoln's suffrage proposal was less democratic than what Illinois law then mandated. By 1836 Lincoln may have read Thomas Paine's *Rights of Man* (1791), but Lincoln had not read Mary Wollstonecraft's *A Vindication of the Rights of Woman* (1792).[87] While Lincoln may not have become a radical democrat while in New Salem, he did begin his commitment to the "cause of reason" there.[88]

In January 1838, Lincoln ended his address on the perpetuation of republican institutions with a call for "reason, cold, calculating, unimpassioned reason."[89]

His 1836 statement on suffrage also came at a time when Lincoln was immersed in his law studies; one of his New Salem neighbors remembers how Lincoln "read hard—day & night—terribly hard.[90] Reading legal treatises would have reinforced Lincoln's commitment to reason. The antebellum period saw an enormous growth in the publication of treatises and a concomitant rise in a "deep and mystical devotion to the proposition that law was a science and that most of its basic problems could be solved through the intense application of reason."[91]

"It's Easy to See Why Ladies Are Whigs"

The Whig campaign in 1840 introduced "a dramatic departure from previous campaigns" because women participated in political events.[92] In Virginia, for example, Whigs made a concerted effort to win the allegiance of women by inviting them to the party's rallies, speeches, and processions. Historian Elizabeth Varon called their outreach an appeal to "Whig womanhood," the notion that women could make vital contributions to party politics. Whig womanhood, as Varon put it, "attempted to reconcile women's partisanship as Whigs with the ideology of domesticity or 'true womanhood.'"[93]

Just like Virginia, the Illinois Whigs in 1840 held "dinners, barbecues, picnics, and processions, with women as spectators and participants."[94] The *Sangamo Journal* reported that a "loco foco" admitted that "it's easy to see why ladies are whigs."[95] (Loco-focos were members of a radical faction of the Democratic Party, but Whigs derogatorily called every Democrat a Loco-foco.) The "Whig ladies" presented flags to county delegations and participated in dinners, rallies, and log cabin raisings.[96] When the Whig state convention met in June, the delegates adopted a resolution recognizing female support: "Resolved, That the spirit and enthusiasm which has been manifested by the ladies on this occasion, and on our various routes to this place, give undoubted evidence that they are animated by the same Whig principles which burned in the breasts of our grandmothers in the times of the Revolution."[97] The participation of Illinois's Whig ladies would be even more pronounced during the 1844 presidential election, when Henry Clay was the Whig candidate.

One of the Whig ladies of Springfield in 1840 was Mary Todd. She was spotted at the *Sangamo Journal* office, "where some fifteen or twenty ladies were collected together to listen to the Tippecanoe Singing Club."[98] During the fall campaign, Todd confessed to her friend Mercy Levering that she had become "quite a *politician*, rather an unladylike profession, yet at such a *crisis*, whose heart could remain untouched while the energies of all were in question?"[99] As a teenager, Todd was described by a family member as "a violent little Whig."[100]

Lincoln first met Mary Todd in Springfield in the winter of 1839, at the beginning of the 1840 presidential campaign, and their courtship began. Todd knew Henry Clay from childhood as a family friend, which would have been very alluring to Clay acolyte Lincoln. Lincoln and Todd's courtship—or engagement—ended but resumed in the summer of 1842, in time for another election season. Politics helped restore their romance.[101] Todd wrote one of the pseudonymous "Lost Township" letters that lampooned Democratic politician James Shields. Lincoln's satirical contribution led to his duel with Shields.[102] Lincoln and Todd were married in November 1842. Mary Lincoln continued to be interested in politics and advised her husband on politics. Her invasion into the male sphere of politics, according to historian Jean Baker, "became the most notable feature of her marriage." But, as First Lady, Mary would still insist that her "character is wholly domestic."[103]

* * *

In 1836 Abraham Lincoln advocated limiting suffrage to whites who paid taxes or served in the militia, which included women who paid taxes. Lincoln was either out of step or misinformed when he called for limiting suffrage to only those who contributed to government in a state where the constitution had already established universal white male suffrage. Lincoln was more conservative, if not reactionary, when compared with the rest of his Whig colleagues in Illinois. Perhaps Lincoln's reading of excerpts of the 1821 New York Constitutional

Convention, which appeared regularly in the *Sangamo Journal*, put him in a somewhat retrograde frame of mind. His proposal for limiting suffrage to taxpayers and militia members was ironically similar to Van Buren's 1821 position that had been savaged by Whigs.[104] Since Lincoln probably wrote some of the very articles in the *Sangamo Journal* that condemned Van Buren for not advocating universal white male suffrage, his public position is even more perplexing.

CHAPTER TWO

LINCOLN KNEW SOMETHING

Lincoln always opposed nativism. Because he saw American citizenship as founded on the principles expressed in the Declaration of Independence, he believed that all white men who accepted that creed had an equal claim to American citizenship. Both native-born and naturalized citizens should be members of the political community.

Whigs and Nativism

Nativist organizations in the 1840s and 1850s pressed for restrictions on the voting rights of immigrants, advocating for changes to state voting laws that would lengthen the time needed for naturalized citizens to vote. The federal naturalization statute in effect at the time permitted "any alien, being a free white person" to become a citizen after residing in the United States for five years, establishing good moral character, and taking an oath supporting the Constitution and renouncing all allegiance to everywhere else the person had previously been a citizen or subject. Aliens did not have to be able to speak English or be able to read to become a citizen.[1] Nativists called for a fourteen-year or twenty-one-year period after naturalization before a foreign-born citizen would become eligible to vote. They also called for bans on holding office by the foreign-born and for literacy tests for immigrants seeking to vote.[2]

While many Whigs were nativists, nativism was more prevalent among Whigs in the Northeast than with Whigs in the Midwest.[3]

Midwestern Whigs were more likely to see immigrants as a driver of economic development since a growing economy needed immigrant workers.[4]

Democrats in Illinois regularly charged Whigs with anti-immigrant and anti-Catholic bias. Whig newspapers and politicians spent a lot of time rebutting charges of nativism and considerable time accusing Democrats of being the real nativists. In 1844, after nativist riots erupted in Philadelphia between Protestants and Catholics, Lincoln and his fellow Springfield Whigs met to answer charges by Democrats that Whigs were responsible for the riots because of their "supposed hostility" to "foreigners and Catholics." The assembled Whigs passed several resolutions denying they were anti-immigrant or anti-Catholic. They stated their opposition to any changes in the naturalization laws that would "render admission under them, less convenient, less cheap, or less expeditious."[5]

Significantly, these resolutions rejected nativist proposals to increase the residency period for citizenship. (The American Republican Party in June 1843, for instance, had proposed extending a five-year residency to twenty-one years.)[6] A writer for the *Illinois State Register*, the Democratic newspaper in Springfield, noted how "Mr. Lincoln expressed the kindest, and most benevolent feelings towards foreigners; they were, I doubt not, the sincere and honest sentiments of *his heart*; but they were not those of *his party*."[7] Lincoln, in fact, was responsible for the Illinois Whig Party adopting these resolutions at the state convention later that summer. As a member of the resolutions committee, Lincoln ensured that the Springfield resolutions were reported to the convention, which then did "concur in the sentiments" of the Springfield Whigs on "the rights of *foreigners* and *Catholics*."[8]

Despite Lincoln's best efforts, most immigrants in Springfield in the 1840s associated Whigs with nativism. Whigs paid dearly for this perception, as immigrants aligned strongly with Democrats. In 1848 about 70 percent of foreign-born voters in Springfield voted Democratic. One-quarter of all Democratic voters were foreign-born, while only one-tenth of Whig voters were immigrants. Irish and German voters favored Democrats by a three-to-one margin.[9]

The End of Alien Voting

Whereas the Constitution gave the federal government exclusive authority over naturalization, states decided who could vote. Illinois was one of several states that permitted immigrants to vote before they became naturalized. Its constitution stated that "inhabitants"—not citizens—were eligible to vote, and noncitizens regularly voted in elections. Although there were solid reasons why this practice of allowing noncitizens to vote might be problematic, Whigs only began fretting about alien voting when they started losing elections because alien voters voted heavily Democratic. For the 1838 loss of their candidate for governor and the razor-thin victory of Whig John T. Stuart over Democrat Stephen Douglas for US Congress, the Whigs blamed bloc voting by Irish canal workers.[10] When Lincoln wrote John T. Stuart about the possibility of holding elections for the Twenty-Seventh Congress in the summer of 1840, he said that Whigs thought canal construction and other public works would be stopped by the summer, "and consequently, we shall then be clear of the foreign votes, whereas by another year they may be brought in again."[11]

After the August 1838 elections, the *Sangamo Journal* published several articles on immigrant voters. One article warned that immigrants from the different kingdoms of Europe had poured into the United States and that, in Illinois, they were working as laborers on public works like the Illinois and Michigan Canal. These canal workers were predominantly Irish, and "instead of becoming *Americans*, they have brought Ireland with them." While Irish immigrants were criticized, German immigrants were extolled for being a "laborious, enterprising, moral and quiet people," a characterization that Lincoln and other Illinois Republicans would repeat in the 1850s.[12] Whigs—and, later, Republicans—saw German immigrants as settlers who would buy land and farm, and saw Irish immigrants as workers who were low skilled and itinerate.[13]

Stuart won his seat in Congress by only 130 votes out of more than 36,000 votes cast. Lincoln and other Illinois Whigs worried about Douglas contesting the outcome. Lincoln and four other Whigs consequently prepared a form letter that was sent to Whig newspaper editors, stressing the importance of being ready for such a contest. The letter asked the editors to collect the proof necessary to challenge votes for Douglas. It inquired whether any errors had been made in tallying votes from the poll books, whether anyone who voted for Douglas was a minor or had not established residency, and whether "any *unnaturalized foreigners* voted for Mr. Douglass [*sic*] in your County." The third inquiry makes it clear that Lincoln and his colleagues had accepted the Whig argument advanced earlier in the year in a lawsuit filed in Jo Daviess County claiming that the Illinois Constitution did not establish voting by noncitizens.[14]

The outcome of the race between Stuart and Douglas was not known for several weeks, and the *Sangamo Journal* erroneously concluded that Douglas had won by 130 votes. It lamented that Douglas would owe his seat "not to the citizens of this District, but to workmen on our public improvements, not American citizens—who have no fixed place of abode." The article also complained of illegal votes from Irish workers, which would be a common complaint of Illinois Whigs—and, later, Republicans.[15] Whigs complained about Irish canal workers, and Republicans, including Lincoln, would later complain about Irish railroad workers, who allegedly either voted multiple times or had failed to establish residence.

The *Sangamo Journal* continued this campaign against alien voting throughout the fall. In December the *Journal* claimed that it did not object to votes from "[f]oreigners, where they have made themselves citizens of the state." But the Irish canal workers "come in the spring—work during the summer—and leave the state in the fall—many never return. They are transient persons, and neither *citizens* or *inhabitants*."[16]

In 1839 Whigs filed a collusive lawsuit in Jo Daviess County to stop alien voting, hoping to get a favorable decision from the Illinois Supreme Court before the 1840 election. To get the issue before the court, plaintiff Horace Houghton complained that Thomas Spraggins, the Whig election judge, knowingly allowed Jeremiah Kyle, a "native of Ireland" and not a naturalized citizen, to vote in the previous election. Dan Stone, the judge who heard the case, was a former Whig representative to the Illinois General Assembly. Stone held that the election judge violated the law because the defendant was not legally qualified to vote because he was not yet a citizen of the United States.[17]

The case then headed to the Illinois Supreme Court, where it would be heard by a court consisting of three Whigs and one Democrat. Facing what they believed to be certain defeat, the Democrats sought to delay the case at least until after the 1840 elections and also introduced a "court-packing" bill that would increase the size of the court from four to nine justices. The case was continued from the December 1839 term to the June 1840 term, and after Stephen Douglas found an error in the circuit court record, the case was continued again to the following December. That ensured the alien vote would still be allowed in the state and national elections that year.[18]

When the Illinois Supreme Court finally heard the case in the December 1840 term, Theophilus W. Smith, the Democratic judge on the court, wrote a long, discursive opinion holding that the challenged alien voter was legally qualified to vote under the Illinois Constitution because *inhabitant* meant resident. Consequently, voting was not limited to citizens.[19] Apparently hoping to stave off the pending court-packing bill, the three Whig judges surprisingly concurred with the conclusion reached by Smith.[20] After a long and contentious battle, the court-packing bill passed, largely due to Douglas's efforts.[21] Douglas, who was so closely identified with the court-packing bill that it became known as the "Douglas bill," was selected by the legislature to be one of the five new judges on the court. Lincoln's more than seven hundred references to "Judge Douglas" in his speeches in the 1850s were meant pejoratively: Lincoln was reminding his audiences about Douglas's prominent role in the court-packing scheme and his subsequent selection to the court, which foes of Douglas considered a payoff.[22]

While the case was pending in the Illinois Supreme Court, Springfield had moved to incorporate as a city. Because Springfield was a Whig stronghold, Democrats believed that the city's charter was a Whig plot spearheaded by Lincoln and Edward D. Baker.[23] The charter necessarily had to address who could vote in its elections. Other cities had not mentioned citizenship as a requirement for voting in their city charters,[24] but Springfield's charter pointedly stated that voters consisted of "all free white male inhabitants, citizens of the United States."[25] The charter's language on voting codified the Whig argument against alien suffrage, but it also reflected the fact that alien voters in Springfield had unanimously voted Democratic in the 1838 election.[26] The limitation on suffrage in the charter met with some resistance in the legislature but still passed handily. The Sangamon County delegation split its vote four to two, with Lincoln voting in favor of the charter.[27] Voters ratified the charter in the subsequent election in Springfield.[28] The Whig victory on limiting suffrage was short-lived, however. In the wake of the supreme court's ruling on alien voters, the Democratic-controlled legislature amended Springfield's charter in the following session, repealing the citizenship provision and substituting language allowing "every inhabitant" of Springfield "who is entitled to vote for state officers" to vote in city elections.[29]

The 1847 Illinois Constitutional Convention addressed the rights of both noncitizens and naturalized citizens to hold office and to vote.[30] Democratic delegates were quick to label any proposed changes affecting suffrage or elective office as "Native American." The term was used as shorthand for being anti-immigrant and anti-Catholic, and it associated those delegates advocating changes in suffrage with a party widely seen as condoning violence and destruction in the wake of the Philadelphia riots of 1844.[31] The "Native Americans" had first appeared in New York in 1835, running candidates who were anti-Catholic and opposed to the foreign-born holding political offices. That group soon disappeared. In 1843 nativists in New York created the American Republican Party and called for extending the required period of residence for naturalization from five years to twenty-one years and for supporting only native-born citizens for public office. Having won elections in Pennsylvania, Massachusetts, and New York, the American Republicans held a national convention in 1845 in Philadelphia, where they rechristened themselves the Native American Party.[32]

Proponents of changing the suffrage provision argued that the right to vote was linked inextricably to citizenship, as a pair of Illinois

Whig farmers claimed. Gilbert Turnbull argued for the principle that "in any society whatever, members alone have a right to a voice in the management of the affairs of that society. . . . [I]n my opinion, *citizenship, alone*, can entitle a person to vote."[33] Henry Greene claimed a majority of foreigners who came to Illinois were either ignorant or "criminals and paupers," which provided an additional argument in favor of the new provision on suffrage.[34]

Opponents of the suffrage provision gave two general arguments against it. First, it abandoned the "policy of our fathers to encourage immigration from the east, and from foreign lands."[35] Democratic delegate Thompson Campbell stated that Illinois needed immigrants and should continue to hold out "the greatest inducement for men" to come to the state.[36] Opponents also associated the proposed suffrage provision with nativism and, in particular, with the policies of the Native American Party.[37]

The proposed suffrage provision eventually passed. The "foreign voter" provision of the 1818 Illinois Constitution, which allowed "all white male inhabitants above the age of 21" to vote, was supplanted by a new one in the 1848 Constitution, which limited suffrage to "every white male citizen above the age of 21" and "every white male inhabitant" who was residing in the state at the time of the adoption of the constitution. The 1848 Constitution also lengthened the residence requirement from six months to one year.[38]

After the Whigs had taken away alien voting in the new constitution, Democrats argued that the Whigs were nativists bent on taking the right to vote from all immigrants, including naturalized citizens. In 1852 the *Illinois Daily Journal* responded to the *Springfield Register*'s prediction that Whigs would try to prevent "our adopted citizens" from voting. The *Register* had suggested that naturalized citizens not bring their naturalization papers to the polls as a method of preventing challenges to their qualifications for voting. The *Journal* solicited the opinion of Lincoln and two other Whig lawyers, who stated that any person taking the oath was entitled to vote "unless counter proof be made." They further asserted that counterproof could be made by cross-examination and other independent testimony. The *Journal* suggested that "our friends among the adopted citizens" should bring their naturalization papers with them in "case of a controversy." While on the surface the article seemed helpful, it confirmed the *Register*'s point that Whigs would be challenging immigrants at the polls.[39]

Lincoln and the Know-Nothings

The nativist parties of the 1840s had been short-lived. The nativist Know-Nothing Party, however, experienced a spectacular rise and fall. The party began after the 1852 presidential election when nativists lost their faith in the Whig Party as a reliable bulwark against immigration and Catholicism. The Whig Party had sought the support of German and Irish immigrants when its presidential candidate, Winfield Scott, made clumsy and ineffective overtures to foreign-born voters.[40] Nativists felt betrayed by the Whig overtures to immigrants. The Know-Nothing Party was to be steadfastly antislavery, anti-Catholic, and anti-immigrant.

The rise of the Know-Nothings was also fueled by a dramatic increase in immigration. Three million immigrants came to the United States between 1845 and 1854. By 1850, 40 percent of foreign settlers in the United States were Catholics from Ireland.[41]

The Know-Nothing movement reached Illinois in time for the 1854 elections. The party's platform in Illinois called for modifying naturalization laws by extending the residency requirement and repealing any state law that permitted resident aliens to vote, resisting "the corrupting influences and aggressive policy of the Roman Church," and restoring the Missouri Compromise to keep slavery out of the territories.[42] The Know-Nothings operated as a secret fraternal organization, and members used "handgrips, signs, and manner of speech" to safeguard their identity.[43] The secrets apparently were not very well kept. David Davis wrote Lincoln after the election about one Watson, "the secret nominee of the Know Nothings."[44]

When Lincoln had returned to Illinois in 1849 after serving his one term in Congress, he returned to his law practice. He later said he "was losing interest in politics, when the repeal of the Missouri Compromise aroused me again."[45] In 1854 Lincoln reentered the political arena as a candidate for office, running for a seat in the Illinois

General Assembly. Lincoln and Stephen T. Logan, who was also running for state representative as a Whig, each met with an American Party committee in Sangamon County. (The American Party was nicknamed the Know-Nothing Party.) The committee told both Whig politicians that they had been endorsed by the American Party. The committee first met with Logan, and after a "pleasant interview," he "cheerfully accepted" the nomination. Logan subsequently became a leader of the American Party in Illinois.[46] The committee then went to Lincoln's law office to discuss his secret nomination. Lincoln told the group that he still "belonged to the Old Whig party" and would continue to do so "until a better one arose to take its place." He said he would not become identified with the American Party. Its members could vote for him if they wanted, as could the Democrats, but "he was not in sentiment with this new party."[47]

Lincoln needled the delegation about nativists using "Native American" as a label for their beliefs. He rhetorically asked them who the Native Americans were. "Do they not," he said, "wear the breech-clout and carry the tomahawk? We pushed them from their homes and now turn upon others not fortunate enough to come over as early as we or our forefathers. Gentlemen of the committee, your party is wrong on principle." Lincoln was making fun of the group for using the term "Native Americans" when its members were decidedly not Native Americans. The self-styled Native Americans who were critical of European immigrants were themselves descendants of European immigrants. Lincoln then used a story to make his point: "When the Know-nothing party first came up, I had an Irishman, Patrick by name, hoeing in my garden. One morning I was there with him, and he said, 'Mr. Lincoln, what about the Know-nothings?' I explained that they would possibly carry a few elections and disappear, and I asked Pat why he was not born in this country. 'Faith, Mr. Lincoln,' he replied, 'I wanted to be, but my mother wouldn't let me.'"[48] Lincoln's anecdote captured his tolerant attitude toward European immigrants: Lincoln accepted immigrants because their coming to the United States affirmed that they wished to have been born here.[49] Lincoln's skepticism toward all organized religion meant he would not have been receptive to attacking Catholics for not being Protestants.[50] Rejecting the intolerance of the nativists, Lincoln refused the American Party nomination. Not being the secret nominee of the nativists did not hurt Lincoln—both Lincoln and Logan were elected to the legislature.[51]

Even as Lincoln privately criticized the Know-Nothings in letters, he avoided antagonizing them publicly, believing their support was crucial for the anti-Nebraska, anti-Douglas forces. Lincoln also was sometimes disingenuous in public about the Know-Nothings. The Democratic *Illinois State Register* reported Lincoln as saying in a Springfield speech that he "knew nothing of the secret institution."[52] In a speech in Bloomington two weeks later, Lincoln continued in this vein, saying that "he *Knew Nothing* in regard to the Know-Nothings, and he had serious doubts whether such an organization existed." But, he said "in all seriousness," if such an organization really existed and wanted to interfere "with the rights of foreigners," then he was against it as much as Douglas. Still, Lincoln equivocated, "If there was an order styled the Know-Nothings, and there was any thing bad in it, he was unqualifiedly against it; and if there was any thing good in it, why, he said God speed it!"[53]

Lincoln may have been too clever by half. After winning his race for the Illinois legislature, he resigned to run for the US Senate because the election results favored an anti-Nebraska candidate.[54] Lincoln lost his bid for Senate, possibly because he was seen as having Know-Nothing support.[55] One paper announced, "Mr. Lincoln is a Know Nothing and expects the full vote" of the Know-Nothings. Lincoln lost support because of this perceived association, and he refused to denounce the Know-Nothings for fear of losing even more support.[56] Ironically, some Know-Nothings also refused to back Lincoln because he was seen as an old-line Whig.

Lincoln continued to criticize the Know-Nothings privately. In an August 1855 letter to Owen Lovejoy, an abolitionist member of the Illinois legislature, Lincoln discussed the necessity of persuading the Know-Nothings to oppose the extension of slavery without their "Know-nothingism." Lincoln said he was willing to "fuse" with anyone "provided I can fuse on grounds which I think is right." He confided to Lovejoy that "of their principles I think little better than I do of those of the slavery extensionists. Indeed I do not perceive how any one professing to be sensitive to the wrongs of the negroes, can join in a league to degrade a class of white men." In Illinois, Lincoln had wanted the Know-Nothing Party to "die out" without him having to take an open stand against individuals who were "mostly my old political and personal friends."[57]

Lincoln's most famous denunciation of nativism is found in a letter to his friend Joshua Speed, written in the same month as the letter to Lovejoy, in which he responded to Speed's question about where Lincoln stood politically. Lincoln said he thought he was a Whig, "but others say there are no whigs, and that I am an abolitionist." Lincoln did not accept the abolitionist designation because he did "no more than oppose the *extension* of slavery." But Lincoln was sure about one thing: "I am not a Know-Nothing." He explained:

> How could I be? How can anyone who abhors the oppression of negroes, be in favor of degrading classes of white people? Our progress in degeneracy appears to me to be pretty rapid. As a nation, we began by declaring that "*all men are created equal.*" We now practically read it "all men are created equal, *except negroes.*" When the Know-Nothings get control, it will read "all men are created equal, except negroes, *and foreigners, and catholics.*" When it comes to this I should prefer emigrating to some country where they make no pretence of loving liberty—to Russia, for instance, where despotism can be taken pure, and without the base alloy of hypocracy.[58]

Lincoln was not yet ready to criticize Know-Nothings publicly because he wanted them to join the anti-Nebraska forces.

The Election of 1856

Other Republicans in Illinois began publicly criticizing Know-Nothings before Lincoln did. The Republicans in Chicago adopted a platform of principles in November 1855 that held the "only true rule" for office was "merit, not birth place" and that naturalization laws should not be changed because "we should welcome the exiles and emigrants from the Old World, to homes of enterprise and of freedom in the new."[59]

By the early months of 1856, Lincoln was ready both to join the Republican Party and to criticize the nativists. He helped draft an anti-nativist plank at an 1856 meeting of antislavery newspaper editors in Decatur, which Lincoln attended as an informal guest. When the anti-nativist plank introduced by German immigrant George Schneider met with opposition, Theodore Canisius recalled Lincoln saying that "we must state our position honestly and openly, and only through an unqualified proclamation can we count on support. The citizens who have adopted this country as their own have a right to demand this from us."[60] Lincoln said the anti-nativist plank was "nothing new. It is already contained in the Declaration of Independence." The plank borrowed the language of the Chicago Republicans.[61] At the Republican convention in Bloomington in May, the newly formed party adopted a platform that held "the spirit of our institutions as well as the Constitution of our country, guarantees the liberty of conscience as well as political freedom, and that we will proscribe no one by legislation or otherwise on account of religious opinions, or in consequence of place of birth."[62] The Republicans, like Lincoln, were ready to fuse with Know-Nothings so long as they did not bring "Know-Nothingism."

The 1856 presidential election pitted James Buchanan, the Democratic Party nominee, against John C. Frémont, the Republican Party candidate, and Millard Fillmore, the Know-Nothing nominee. Lincoln accurately foresaw that the anti-Nebraska vote in Illinois would be split by Frémont and Fillmore, which would assure Buchanan a win of the state's electoral votes. Lincoln sent a lithographed form letter to "good, steady Fillmore men" that tried to convince Fillmore supporters in Illinois to shift their support tactically to Frémont if they wanted to help their candidate nationally. Otherwise, Buchanan "*will get Illinois*, if men persist in throwing away votes upon Mr. Fillmore." Lincoln cautioned them that if Buchanan won Illinois, he would win the election, but Lincoln's plea fell on deaf ears: Buchanan won Illinois with 44 percent of the vote, while Frémont received 40 percent and Fillmore, 16 percent.[63]

Illinois had ended alien voting for immigrants who arrived in Illinois after the adoption of the new state constitution; however, the suffrage provision retained the previous term *inhabitant* for residents who were living in Illinois at the time of the adoption of the constitution. Lincoln, in an unsigned 1856 editorial published in a Galena newspaper, took the time to explain this unusual compromise after a Democratic newspaper had asserted that noncitizens could not legally vote in Illinois. "This is a grave error," Lincoln wrote. "Our Legislature *has* directed, that unnaturalized foreigners, who were here before the adoption of our late State Constitution, shall, in common with others, vote for and appoint Presidential Electors." Lincoln was on the side of these "unnaturalized foreigners" in Illinois. "Let not this class of foreigners be alarmed," he affirmed. "Our Legislature has directed that they may vote for Electors; and the U.S. Constitution has expressly authorized the Legislature to make that direction."[64]

Nativism and the Senate Race of 1858

The Republicans in Illinois succeeded in absorbing former Know-Nothings without absorbing what Lincoln called "Know-Nothing-ism."[65] Democrats rarely attacked Lincoln, the Republican standard-bearer in 1858, or the Republicans for supporting nativism. Stephen Douglas never tried to paint Lincoln a Know-Nothing in their debates, probably because Douglas had decided to win over Know-Nothings by positing a battle between "Fremont abolitionism on the one side and constitutional-law-abiding-Union-loving men under the Democratic banner on the other side."[66]

Lincoln gave the fullest expression of his vision of a white republic that included both native-born and naturalized citizens during the US Senate campaign. Unlike those white Anglo-Saxon Protestants who believed themselves to be the foundation of American greatness, Lincoln believed American greatness grew from the principles of the Declaration of Independence. Any European immigrant who came to the United States because of the promise of the Declaration was already sufficiently "Americanized." Lincoln never worried about whether immigrants would assimilate because a belief in the principles of the Declaration would unify all Americans, native and foreign-born. The Declaration was the "electric cord" that links "the hearts of patriotic and liberty-loving men together." Lincoln explained in a campaign speech in July that it did not matter whether these men "descended by blood from our ancestors" or were recent arrivals from Europe. As long as the Declaration of Independence was "the father of all moral principle in them," they had a right to claim it "as though they were blood of the blood, and flesh of the flesh of the men who wrote [it.]"[67]

Lincoln believed that Europeans would be attracted to America's promise of an "equal chance" given to all. He welcomed all immigrants from Europe, making no distinctions between those who were of Anglo-Saxon stock and those who were not. In this respect, he differed from many in the Whig Party, some in the Republican Party, and everyone in the Know-Nothing Party. Lincoln presented his vision of "free soil, free labor, free men" in the territories in his last debate with Douglas. The territories would be "an outlet for free white people everywhere," not just those "born amongst us." Lincoln welcomed "Hans and Baptiste and Patrick and all other men from all the world" in seeking to "find new homes and better their conditions in life."[68]

Lincoln did not mention, though, that the Declaration of Independence had different meanings for black and white people. For blacks, the Declaration posited that all men were created equal and had the same natural rights. For whites, the Declaration became an "electric cord" that tied "the hearts of patriotic and liberty-loving men together," whether they were descendants of the "iron men" who fought for independence or had come from Europe after the Revolutionary War was won. Celebrating the Fourth of July allowed all these men to feel more attached to one another, "more firmly bound to the country we inhabit." Adhering to the same principles allowed all white men—native-born or not—to be part of this "mighty nation." Even though members of Lincoln's imagined community were linked together only by belief in the principles of the Declaration, Lincoln was only talking about immigrants from Europe ("men who have come from Europe—German, Irish, French and Scandinavian"). Lincoln did not recognize black men as patriotic and liberty-loving until the Civil War. It was only then that at least some blacks could be considered part of this "mighty nation."[69]

It is not clear whether Lincoln would have included Asians or Mexicans as being part of the political community with white men through a common allegiance to the principles of the Declaration. In 1859, when Lincoln extolled the virtues of "Young America," he remarked that "in civilization, and the arts, the people of Asia are entirely behind those of Europe." He also pointed out how "yankees, almost instantly" discovered gold in California, "which had been trodden upon, and over-looked by indians and Mexican greasers, for centuries."[70] Lincoln had referred to Mexicans as "this race of mongrels" the year before in a debate with Douglas.[71] There's no record of Lincoln addressing the arrival of Chinese immigrants in California in the 1850s, an arrival met by a series of hostile laws passed by the State of California.[72] Nor did Lincoln comment on a provision in the Treaty of Guadalupe Hidalgo that permitted Mexicans living in lands acquired by the United States to choose to become American citizens.[73]

Lincoln's "invisible community" bound together by the principles of the Declaration of Independence could include American Indians provided they assimilated.[74] Lincoln believed Indians were savages inclined to violence.[75] He explained to a group of Native Americans gathered at the White House in March 1863 the "great difference between this pale-faced people and their red brethren": whites were "numerous and prosperous" because they farmed instead of hunted. Moreover, even though whites were "engaged in a great war between one another, we are not, as a race, so much disposed to fight and kill one another as our red brethren." If Native Americans wanted to become "as numerous and prosperous as the white race," then they needed to "adopt a new mode of life"—agriculture.[76] In his annual message to Congress later that year, Lincoln called for the government to assist Native Americans in their "progress in the arts of civilization, and, above all, to that moral training which, under the blessing of Divine Providence, will confer upon them the elevated and sanctifying influences, the hopes and consolation of the Christian faith."[77] Lincoln was continuing the federal "civilization" policy toward Native peoples. This policy used assimilation and citizenship to destroy Native sovereignty, ensuring westward expansion by white settlers.[78] As president, Lincoln carried out the 1860 platform of the Republican Party, which promised settlement of the West.

Lincoln was particularly solicitous toward German immigrants. His law partner William Herndon later recalled that Lincoln "had no prejudices against any class, preferring the Germans to any foreign element, yet tolerating—as I never could—even the Irish."[79] After 1851 Germans had replaced the Irish as the largest incoming group. The German-born population in the United States grew from 584,720 to 1,301,136 in 1860. By 1850 there were 38,451 German immigrants in Illinois, a sizable percentage (4.5 percent) in a state with a total population of 851,470. The German-born population in Illinois reached 130,804 (7.6 percent) in 1860, when Illinois had a total population of 1,711,951.[80] Germans were the largest immigrant group in the Republican Party. Gustave Koerner, a German immigrant and Illinois politician, recalled Lincoln speaking in Belleville during the 1856 campaign. Lincoln told the Belleville crowd that everywhere he spoke "he had found the Germans more enthusiastic for the cause of freedom than all other nationalities." Nearly in tears, Lincoln exclaimed, "God bless the Dutch!" (Americans had referred to Germans as Dutch, from *Deutsch*, since the 1740s.)[81]

One of the reasons Republican politicians in the Midwest disavowed anti-immigrant policies was to garner votes from Germans.[82] During the 1858 US Senate campaign, Lincoln called for German speakers to be sent across the state and helped arrange the publication of his speeches in German. He warned Gustave Koerner that the party was "in great danger" in Madison County and asked if Koerner, the newspaper editor Theodore Canisius, "and some other influential Germans set a plan on foot that shall gain us accession from the Germans, and see that, at the election, none are cheated in their ballots."[83]

While Lincoln publicly welcomed "Hans and Baptiste and Patrick," he harbored some suspicion about Patrick. Irish voters generally supported the Democratic Party; Lincoln once alluded to Irish immigrants as "those adopted citizens, whose votes have given Judge Douglas all his consequence."[84] While Lincoln worked hard to get votes from German immigrants, he expressed concern over fraudulent voting by

Irish laborers, echoing Whig concerns about illegal voting by Irish canal workers in 1838. In September Lincoln wrote Norman B. Judd that he was cautiously optimistic about his race with Douglas "unless they overcome us by fraudulent voting." Lincoln said that the Republicans had to be "especially prepared for this," and the prospect of fraudulent voting "must be taken into anxious consideration at once." Lincoln thought they could defeat voting fraud if it consisted of "men imported from other states and men not naturalized." He was more worried about another type of fraud: otherwise "qualified Irish voters of Chicago" being deployed to a "doubtful district, having them to swear to an actual residence when they offer to vote." Lincoln warned that voter fraud was "a great danger, and we must all attend to it."[85]

Lincoln sometimes stated his concerns about illegal voting by Irish workers out loud. A Democratic paper reported that Lincoln grumbled in a speech about his seeing "about a dozen Irishmen on the levee, and it occurred to him that those Irishmen had been imported expressly to vote him down." The paper was outraged by Lincoln's suggestion: "Doubtless Mr. Lincoln entertains a holy horror of all Irishmen and other adopted citizens who have sufficient self-respect to believe themselves superior to the negro." The paper charged that Lincoln's expressed fear was a cue to his followers to keep "adopted citizens" from the polls.[86]

Nativism and Massachusetts

Massachusetts was a stronghold of the Know-Nothing Party, which swept state elections in 1854. The Know-Nothing governor, Henry J. Gardner, proposed a twenty-one-year waiting period *after naturalization* before immigrants could vote. This proposal, along with a literacy test for voting, passed the legislature in 1855. Under the terms of the Massachusetts Constitution, it had to pass two successive legislatures before it would be put before the electorate. In 1856 the legislature instead substituted a fourteen-year period. In the 1857 legislature, now dominated by Republicans, the fourteen-year period was defeated and a two-year period substituted. The two-year period passed again in 1858. The measure was then placed before the voters for approval. Lincoln was one of many western Republicans who opposed the two-year period, worried that the provision would hinder the party's ability to appeal to immigrant voters, particularly Germans.[87]

Lincoln prepared a resolution for the Illinois Republican Party condemning the Massachusetts legislature for approving the two-year period, and after the provision was passed, Theodore Canisius asked Lincoln if he supported it. Lincoln conceded that "Massachusetts is a sovereign and independent state; and it is no privilege of mine to scold her for what she does." But he was more than willing to state his opposition to such a provision in Illinois "or in any other place, where I have a right to oppose it." Lincoln explained: "Understanding the spirit of our institutions to aim at the *elevation* of men, I am opposed to whatever tends to *degrade* them. I have some little notoriety for commiserating the oppressed condition of the negro; and I should be strangely inconsistent if I could favor any project for curtailing the existing rights of *white men*, even though born in different lands, and speaking different languages from myself."[88] Canisius published the letter in the German-language *Illinois Staats-Anzeiger* and in the *Illinois State Journal*.[89]

Lincoln understood that nativist appeals were politically damaging in the Midwest. In an 1859 letter, he decried Republicans' tendency to include issues that were popular in their own state but a "firebrand" elsewhere. As an example, he lamented that "Massachusetts republicans should have looked beyond their noses; and then they could not have failed to see that tilting against foreigners would ruin us in the whole North-West."[90]

The Campaign of 1860

Before the 1860 presidential campaign, Lincoln bought a printing press for Canisius to start a German paper in Springfield that would adhere to the "Philadelphia and Illinois Republican platforms."[91] The Republican Party platform in 1860 included a pro-immigration plank that repudiated the Massachusetts residency provision. Koerner and Carl Schurz were on the platform committee and fought hard for the language, which stated that the Republican Party was "opposed to any change in our naturalization laws, or any state legislation by which the rights of citizenship hitherto accorded to emigrants from foreign lands shall be abridged or impaired; and in favor of giving a full and efficient protection to the rights of all classes of citizens, whether native or naturalized, both at home and abroad."[92]

When the Pennsylvania and Indiana delegations met at the 1860 Republican National Convention to discuss which candidate to support, supporters of Edward Bates showed up in force. Bates, a former Whig and Know-Nothing from Missouri, was one of the main contenders for the Republican nomination. (Bates would later serve as Lincoln's attorney general.) The Lincoln-supporting Illinois delegation sent Koerner, a former Democrat, and Orville H. Browning, a former Whig, to counteract the Bates movement. Koerner told the delegations that Bates had supported Know-Nothings in municipal elections in Missouri and that German Republicans would never vote for Bates. Browning observed that "on the other hand Lincoln had always opposed Native Americanism. This would secure him the foreign Republican vote all over the country."[93]

After Lincoln secured the nomination, campaign literature highlighted his pro-immigration views. In its first edition the Chicago *Rail Splitter* reprinted Lincoln's letter to Canisius with the headline "Mr. Lincoln on Naturalization."[94] The Freeport *Wide Awake* on the eve of the election proclaimed that Lincoln was gaining thousands of votes from Germans in New York because "they can't stand the Douglas fusion with the Know Nothings" and that the Irish in Illinois also would be voting for Lincoln.[95] Other Republican newspapers throughout the North published the Canisius letter.[96] Lincoln associated America with freedom and Europe with despotism. European immigrants were fleeing from "oppression of tyranny" and heading to "the land of their adoption."[97]

Lincoln consistently rejected nativist proposals to make it more difficult for immigrants to naturalize or to vote. He was outspoken in 1844 after anti-Catholic riots in Philadelphia and in 1859 when Massachusetts nativists proposed lengthening the time that aliens had to wait after naturalization before they were permitted to vote. Lincoln was more circumspect in criticizing Know-Nothings in Illinois because he wanted them to join the Republican Party. He wanted this "fusion" on his terms: he wanted Know-Nothings without Know-Nothingism.

CHAPTER THREE

A WHITE MAN'S REPUBLIC

Until 1865 Lincoln's imagined community of citizenship did not include black men. Lincoln was antislavery, but he was not an abolitionist. Rejecting both slavery and abolitionism, Lincoln chose a "moderate" course that supported repressive laws for free blacks in Illinois and advocated colonization of blacks in Liberia.

The Illinois Black Laws

Among northern states, the states in the Midwest were those most firmly committed to white supremacy, and of those, Illinois was the most racist.[1] Illinois, Frederick Douglass noted, was "facetiously called a free state."[2] First as a territory and then as a state, Illinois permitted slavery and a form of quasi-slavery based on indentures. Like other midwestern states, it passed a series of statutes commonly called Black Laws that denied social and political rights to free black people. In 1848 whites in Illinois added a provision to their state's constitution that prohibited blacks from settling there.[3]

The Black Laws did not make Illinois lily-white, but they may have had some impact. The number of black residents in the state grew from 2,384 in 1830 to 7,628 in 1860, but the exponential growth of the white population meant that the percentage of black Illinoisans shrank from 1.5 percent in 1830 to 0.4 percent in 1860.[4] The black population in Springfield was approximately 26 (out of a total population of 1,500) when Lincoln arrived in 1837 and had grown to 234 (out of a total population of 9,320) when Lincoln left Springfield in 1861.[5]

Throughout his political career in Illinois, Lincoln never took any position inconsistent with the state's Black Laws. In 1858 he alluded to the Black Laws as "the necessities that spring from the actual presence of black people amongst us."[6] After Lincoln's election to president, the abolitionist Wendell Phillips accurately summarized Lincoln's views on the rights of black people:

> Do you believe, Mr. Abraham Lincoln, that the negro is your political and social equal, or ought to be? Not a bit of it.
> Do you believe he should sit on juries? Never.
> Do you think he should vote? Certainly not.
> Should he be considered a citizen? I tell you frankly, no.
> Do you think that, when the Declaration of Independence says, "All men are created equal," it intends the political equality of blacks and whites? No, sir.[7]

Lincoln's support for Illinois's Black Laws—and obvious lack of support for black citizenship—did not go unnoticed during the presidential campaign of 1860. Black abolitionist H. Ford Douglas, who lived in Illinois, attacked Lincoln and the Republican Party in several speeches later published in the abolitionist press.[8] Douglas criticized Lincoln for his support of "a code of laws that would disgrace any Barbary State."[9] Lincoln opposed "the rights of the free colored people, even in his own state," and "shuts them out from the courts of justice." Douglas argued that Lincoln endorsed "even the worst features of that infamous [*Dred Scott*] decision, 'that the black man has no rights which the white man is bound to respect.'" Illinois law prohibited Douglas from testifying against a white man in court. That meant that "any villain may enter my house in Chicago and outrage my family, and unless a white man stands by to see it done, I have no redress."[10] And if a white man "happens to owe me anything, unless I can prove it by the testimony of a white man, I cannot collect the debt."[11]

Douglas described how he had implored Republican leaders in Illinois to support the repeal of the testimony law "so as to permit colored men to testify against white men."[12] Douglas had approached prominent Republicans like Lincoln and US Senator Lyman Trumbull and asked them to sign a repeal petition. Lincoln refused to do so.

Trumbull not only refused but also told Douglas that if he "did not like the laws of Illinois," then he "had better leave the state!"[13] Although Douglas's appeal was rejected by Lincoln and Trumbull, Republicans in the Illinois General Assembly unsuccessfully attempted to repeal the testimony law in 1859.[14]

Douglas's critique was not finished. He also wondered why an antislavery man would support a party that did not support his right to vote. He explained, "I am a colored man; I am an American citizen, and I think that I am entitled to exercise the elective franchise." Douglas recounted how Lincoln had reacted in Ohio in 1859 when "the colored people were agitating the question of suffrage in that state."[15] A Democratic newspaper in Columbus asserted that Lincoln had "declared in favor of Negro suffrage, and attempted to defend that vile conception against the Little Giant [Stephen A. Douglas]."[16] Lincoln, the abolitionist Douglas accurately observed, "took pains" to deny this allegation.[17]

Douglas pointed out that Illinois added further insult to injury: it taxed "colored people for every conceivable purpose." Black people were taxed to support schools for the education of "the white man's children, but the colored people are not permitted to enjoy any of the benefits resulting from that taxation." Illinois stole the hard-won earnings of black men to educate white children, and if blacks were to send their children to school, "Abraham Lincoln would kick them out."[18]

Understanding Lincoln's views on black citizenship starts with understanding the laws in Illinois that denied black people political and civil rights. Article 6 of the Northwest Ordinance of 1787 stated that "there shall be neither slavery nor involuntary servitude" in the territory.[19] But in the portion of the territory that would later become Illinois, there were already slaves. Territorial governors considered the ordinance to be prospective only; they allowed French settlers to keep their slaves during both the territorial period and in statehood.[20] White southerners also subsequently brought slaves into the territory. With the division of the Indiana Territory in 1807, the Illinois territorial government soon passed its own laws that allowed slaves to enter but that prohibited free blacks from entering the territory.[21]

The territorial government of Illinois passed an exclusion, or anti-immigration, law in 1813, which bluntly proclaimed it unlawful for "any free negro or mullatto to migrate in this territory." It empowered any citizen to apprehend and bring any interloper before a justice of the peace. The justice of the peace would then give "such free negro or Mullatto" fifteen days to leave the territory. If the person did not voluntarily self-deport, then the justice of the peace would order the migrant "to be whipped on his or her bare back" for twenty-five to thirty-nine stripes. Free blacks and mulattoes already residing in the territory would have to apply to the county court "to be registered and numbered by the clerks," specifying "the name, age, color, and stature of said free negro or mullatto."[22]

In 1814 the territorial government established a subterfuge to permit enslaved people to work in the saltworks. The legislature found that the manufacture of salt could not be "successfully carried on by white laborers," which necessitated the use of slaves—not free black laborers—to do the work. A slave could "voluntarily hire himself or herself, within the Territory, by the consent of his or her master" for one-year terms. To ensure that the slave was giving voluntary consent to the indenture, a justice of the peace or clerk of the court was to examine the slave privately. The impossibility for a slave to "voluntarily hire" out for labor was not addressed directly, but the law stated that such hiring did not operate "in any way whatever to injure the right of property in the master."[23]

Article 6 of the 1818 Illinois Constitution stated, "Neither slavery nor involuntary servitude shall hereafter be introduced into this state." The *hereafter* was doing a lot of work in that sentence. It meant that slaves currently in the territory would not be affected by the new constitution. Moreover, that same article also permitted quasi-slavery for males under age twenty-one and females under eighteen. If a male was over twenty-one or a female was over eighteen, then he or she could become an indentured servant if the indenture was entered into "while in a state of perfect freedom, and on a condition of a bona fide consideration." Indentures "hereafter made" would be limited to one-year terms, conveniently leaving out previously executed indentures, which had ranged from thirty to ninety years.[24]

After Illinois gained statehood in 1818, the state's first general assembly wasted little time before passing a comprehensive set of repressive laws aimed at discouraging African Americans from settling inside state borders and at denying virtually all political and civil rights to those who did. Among other features, no black or "mulatto person" would be permitted to reside in Illinois without obtaining a certificate of "actual freedom" from a judge or court clerk. To prevent masters from emancipating older slaves in Illinois, $1,000 bonds were required to prevent those so emancipated from becoming a charge to any county. If anyone hired a black or mulatto person who did not have his or her freedom certificate, then the employer would have to pay a fine of $1.50 per day. Harboring a runaway slave or preventing the lawful owner from retaking his slave was deemed a felony. If a black or mulatto person was discovered to be without a certificate of freedom, then a justice of the peace would commit the "supposed runaway" person to the custody of the sheriff and advertise a description of the presumed runaway in the nearest newspaper for six weeks. The sheriff's duty was to hire out the undocumented person at "the best price he can get." If no owner appeared within a year, then the black or mulatto person could obtain a certificate of freedom.[25]

The Illinois legislature borrowed liberally from southern slave codes, even keeping such language as "plantation." The Black Laws contained provisions for "any slave or servant" found more than ten miles from his master's residence without a pass to be punished with a whipping of no more than thirty-five stripes, ordered by the justice of the peace. If any slave or servant "presumed" to visit any "plantation" or dwelling without leave from his or her master, then the owner of the plantation or dwelling could administer "ten lashes on his or her bare back." Another provision fined any person who permitted three or more slaves or "servants of color" to assemble for "the purpose of dancing or reveling." The assembled slaves or servants could be whipped up to thirty-nine lashes.[26]

Before the Civil War, Illinois added more repressive measures to its Black Laws. Illinois was one of five free states that prohibited black people from testifying against whites in court.[27] In 1857 Lincoln stated, "There is a natural disgust in the minds of nearly all white people, to the idea of an indiscriminate amalgamation of the white and black races." The Illinois legislature had codified this "natural disgust" in 1845 by prohibiting marriages between a "person of color, negro or mulatto" and a white person.[28]

Furthermore, in the summer of 1847, Illinois held another constitutional convention, and it resulted in a constitutional provision that prohibited black people from entering Illinois. Whig delegate Benjamin Bond of Clinton County requested a report from the Bill of Rights Committee on a "clause prohibiting free negroes from emigrating" into Illinois and prohibiting slaves from being freed in the state.[29] Bond argued that the "class of unfortunate individuals, called free negroes," had become an annoyance. Bond asserted that differences between white and black people prevented them from coexisting in a free society. It was pointless to allow any persons to settle in Illinois "unless they came with right to be our equals in all things, and as freemen." It was no use to give blacks "the privileges of the ballot box" or "all the rights of freemen and citizens of a free republic." Bond alluded to the "objects of colonization" as the solution to the problem of free blacks."[30] Many Whig delegates expressed support for an exclusion provision. For example, Edward M. West, a Whig delegate from Madison County, stated that "free negroes living amongst our people was a great evil"; blacks were "idle and worthless people," and his constituents were anxious to "get rid of them."[31]

Some delegates had abolitionist leanings. Although heavily outnumbered, they made their voices heard. Selden Church, a Whig from Winnebago County, disagreed that "the privileges of common humanity" should not be extended to black people. The exclusion proposal was against "the spirit of the age" and would cause Illinoisans to be "objects of scorn to the world."[32] Archibald Williams, a Whig delegate from Adams County, thought the $1,000 bond requirement was sufficient to prevent blacks from becoming a burden to the state; after giving security, they should be permitted "the poor privilege of cultivating our soil and breathing our air." Several delegates had referred to blacks as a "degraded race." Williams countered that they were degraded because "they had been raised in servitude and without education."[33]

The exclusion clause passed 87 to 55. Democrats overwhelmingly favored the provision by a vote of 65 to 11, and Whigs opposed it 44 to 22.[34] The popular vote was even more lopsided. In March 1848, the new constitution was ratified by a count of 60,585 to 15,903 votes. The "negro article" had a separate vote and passed with 10,000 fewer votes. The exclusion clause passed in 87 of the state's 101 counties, losing in northeastern counties and passing overwhelmingly in southern areas.[35] Statewide, 70 percent of voters supported the provision; in Springfield, it won 84 percent of the vote. Ninety-two percent of Democrats supported the exclusion article, while 80 percent of Whigs supported the measure.[36] Illinois became the first northern state with an exclusion provision in its constitution; Indiana and Oregon later followed suit.[37]

The exclusion clause mandated that the Illinois legislature, at the first session under the new constitution, pass the laws necessary for prohibiting free black people from entering the state and for preventing the owners of enslaved people from freeing them in Illinois. The legislature was unable to comply with either mandate for the first two assemblies under the new constitution. It was not until 1853, in the Eighteenth General Assembly, that the black exclusion law was passed.

The "Act to prevent the immigration of free negroes into this state" addressed both the freeing of enslaved people in Illinois by their masters and the immigration of free black people into Illinois. To prevent manumission, the law prohibited any person from bringing into the state "any negro or mulatto slave, whether said slave is set free or not." Violations would be punished with fines of no less than $100 and no more than $500 and a jail term of no longer than one year. Any black person—"bond or free"—who remained in the state for ten days with the intent to reside would be guilty of a high misdemeanor and fined $50 for the first offense. If the guilty party did not pay the fine, then the justice of the peace would "sell said negro or mulatto" at public auction to someone who would pay the fine and have the guilty party work to pay it off during a "time of service." Once the fine was paid off, the negro or mulatto would have ten days to leave the state or be liable to a second prosecution, with the penalty increasing to $100. If the negro or mulatto was a runaway slave, then the purported slave owner had the right to claim custody of his slave upon presenting proof to the justice of the peace.

When the bill passed the Illinois House of Representatives, A. H. Nixon of McHenry and Boone Counties (Boone County had voted 95 percent against the exclusion clause) moved to amend the title of the bill to "An Act to create an additional number of abolitionists in this state, and for other purposes." His colleague from McHenry and Boone Counties, H. C. Miller moved to amend the amendment by adding "and to assist slaveholders in recovering fugitive slaves."[38]

The exclusion law was the harshest of the Black Laws passed by a northern state.[39] While black exclusion was popular with the voters, the bill received heavy criticism from Illinois newspapers. The *Illinois Daily Journal* stated that most papers were opposed to the law "without reference to party predilections."[40] In a series of articles, the *Journal* excoriated the law as "unjust, inexpedient, unconstitutional and uncalled for."[41] The Democratic *Ottawa Free Trader* asserted that the law established "the Mexican Peon system within our borders—a system of slavery which all admit to be more heartless and cruel than that which exists in our southern States."[42] The *Chicago Democratic Press* claimed that the law was unconstitutional and opposed it because it was "practically changing Illinois from a free into a slave state."[43]

The exclusion law drew national attention as well, with the abolitionist press taking particular interest. Frederick Douglass blasted the "wickedness" of the law: "What kind of people are the people of Illinois? Were they born and nursed of women as other people are? or are they the offspring of wolves and tigers, and only taught to prey upon all flesh pleasing to their bloody taste? . . . Do they look up to God in prayer for mercy? or do they invoke from the foul fiends in the regions of darkness, aid to distress and afflict the helpless who may venture within their reach?"[44] William Lloyd Garrison printed four articles on the Illinois law in the April 1 issue of the *Liberator*. The law was denounced as "infernal legislation" that was "so base, so atrocious" that the devil would realize his services were no longer needed in Illinois.[45]

The Black Laws reflected the deep racism prevalent in Illinois. They also reflected white racial panic. Whites were concerned about maintaining a system of social, political, economic, and legal privilege.[46]

Legal Rights for Black People

Lincoln recognized that black people had some civil rights and believed they were "entitled to all the natural rights enumerated in the Declaration of Independence—the right to life, liberty and the pursuit of happiness." To ensure these natural rights, Lincoln allowed, blacks had to be able to enforce them in court. The right to property—"the right to eat the bread . . . which his own hand earns"—was meaningless without the ability to enforce it in court.[47]

For free black people, the ability to enforce contracts and assert property rights in court was not necessarily guaranteed in the 1850s. For example, Oregon's 1857 Constitution included a black exclusion clause prohibiting any "free negro or mulatto" from holding real estate, making contracts, or maintaining any lawsuit.[48] Other states, however, allowed access to courts. The Kentucky Supreme Court noted in 1820 that "free people of color" were "quasi citizens or, at least, denizens." They were not permitted the "privileges of office and suffrage," but "all other civil and conventional rights are secured to them."[49] Illinois followed Kentucky's approach. The ability to sue or be sued meant that free black people in Illinois, while second-class citizens at best, nonetheless possessed what legal historian Martha S. Jones has called "one of citizenship's hallmark civil rights: the right to protect their persons and property before the law."[50] (The importance of being able to sue in court to enforce contractual and property rights was recognized after the Civil War in the Civil Rights Act of 1866.)[51]

Lincoln's law practice evidences several lawsuits with black litigants, although Lincoln and his partners may have directly represented only six black clients.[52] Most famously, Lincoln represented the legal interests of William Fleurville, who was also known by the sobriquet Billy the Barber, in several matters.[53] He represented Fleurville in a bill to foreclose a mortgage in 1849 and later in a suit for specific performance to require the conveyance of property.[54] In an 1852 letter, Lincoln explained to a Bloomington lawyer that he was "in a little trouble" as he "was trying to get a decree for our 'Billy the Barber' for the conveyance of certain town lots" but had failed to serve the administrator of the estate because of a clerical error. Lincoln said, "Billy will blame me, if I do not get the thing fixed up this time." He asked the lawyer to "sign the authority below" to substitute for service. The court subsequently ordered the property conveyed to Fleurville.[55] Lincoln also served as Fleurville's agent in tax matters.[56]

"I Should Not Know What to Do"

In an 1854 speech in Peoria, Lincoln candidly acknowledged that slavery would be "very difficult to get rid of." He confessed, "If all earthly power were given me, I should not know what to do, as to the existing institution."

He outlined three post-emancipation scenarios if slaves were to be freed immediately. His "first impulse" would be to "free all the slaves, and send them to Liberia,—to their own native land."[57] While Lincoln favored colonization, he realized that if slavery were to end suddenly, then colonization would become an impracticable solution because "its sudden execution is impossible."[58] Moreover, he thought, if black colonists were "all landed there in a day, they would all perish in the next ten days."

If colonization was impracticable, another possibility would be to "free them all, and keep them among us as underlings." Although Lincoln did not explain what he meant by "underlings," he probably meant some form of racial subordination like the Illinois Black Laws. Lincoln asked, "Is it quite certain that this betters their condition?"

That left a third scenario: equality. What about freeing the slaves and then making "them politically and socially, our equals"? Lincoln explained why black citizenship was out of the question: "My own feelings will not admit of this; and if mine would, we well know that those of the great mass of white people will not. Whether this feeling accords with justice and sound judgment, is not the sole question, if indeed, it is any part of it. A universal feeling, whether well or ill-founded, can not be safely disregarded. We can not, then, make them equals."[59]

Lincoln's rejection of black citizenship was based on his feelings and those of other whites. Racism apparently was irrational or, at least, emotionally charged. Lincoln was conceding that black citizenship might be justifiable under notions of "justice and sound judgment." But reason was not enough. This "universal feeling" held by whites could not be "safely disregarded."

Lincoln concluded his thought experiment by stating that some system of gradual emancipation might be adopted.[60] By ending with gradual emancipation, he was circling back to his first impulse, colonization. The Lincoln of the 1850s represented, according to Eric Foner, "the mainstream of white northern opinion, by now convinced that slavery posed a threat to 'free society,' but still convinced of the inherent inferiority of African Americans."[61] These dual beliefs led to widespread—and largely theoretical—support for colonization by white northerners.

Lincoln and Colonization Societies

It is not clear when Lincoln first supported colonization. Whigs tended to support colonization, and Henry Clay, Lincoln's "beau ideal of a statesman," was known for his support for the American Colonization Society, which he helped establish in 1816.[62] But Lincoln's 1849 draft of a gradual emancipation bill for the District of Columbia did not mention colonization of the freed slaves.[63] During his debates with Douglas in 1858, Lincoln said he supported abolishing slavery in the District of Columbia under three conditions, and colonization was not one of them.[64] Lincoln's first public comment about colonization was in 1852, and there is no evidence of his involvement with colonization societies in Springfield before 1853.[65]

Illinois was never a hotbed of the colonization movement. White settlers expressed some interest in colonization when Illinois was still a territory. Later, in 1830, Cyrus Edwards, Ninian Edwards's brother, was able to establish an Illinois State Colonization Society and several local societies in various towns. None of these early attempts lasted. Historian Merton Dillon has suggested that these early colonization societies in Illinois failed because they lacked the funding to be effective; unlike abolition societies, money was needed to make colonization work.[66] From 1832 to 1852, colonization societies in Illinois were responsible for the emigration to Liberia of only thirty-four black people. When the American Colonization Society reported receiving over $80,000 in donations nationally in 1853, Illinoisans had pitched in a paltry $297 (0.37 percent).[67]

As in the rest of the North, colonization societies in Illinois received little support from white abolitionists. White abolitionists like William Lloyd Garrison and Gerrit Smith abandoned their support of colonization in the 1830s, as did white abolitionists in Illinois.[68] In 1837 H. H. Snow discussed the "progress and present prospects" of the American Colonization Society, "showing the utter impracticability of the scheme to effect the emancipation of the colored race" at a meeting of the Adams County Anti-Slavery Society.[69] Soon thereafter, all sides accepted that abolitionism and colonization were antithetical. For example, by 1840 the Whig campaign newspaper in Springfield responded to a report that William Henry Harrison was an abolitionist by merely stating that was not the case because "he is in favor of colonization."[70]

In the 1840s and through most of the 1850s, almost all free black people rejected colonization in Liberia, and most rejected emigration to Central America or Canada.[71] (After the *Dred Scott* decision in 1857, there was increased black interest in emigration; that interest receded after Lincoln issued the Emancipation Proclamation in 1863.)[72] Black opposition to colonization was well known by its white proponents.[73] Since most proponents of colonization advocated voluntary deportation, black resistance was problematic.[74]

Supporters of colonization in Illinois were encouraged when a free black man named S. S. Ball returned to Springfield after visiting Liberia. The Colored Baptist Association sent Ball to Liberia to determine whether that country was more favorable to Illinois's black people than Illinois. After Ball returned, the Illinois Colonization Society claimed that "an increasing disposition is manifest among our colored population, to seek an asylum in the beautiful region from whence their fathers came."[75] But Ball's report likely did not cause much enthusiasm among the Springfield black community. He reported that wealthy colonists were doing well, but there seemed to be "as much distinction made between the rich and poor there, as there is in this country among the whites." Many poor emigrants were "greatly disappointed," as they had expected to be greeted with open arms "and placed upon an equality with the very best families in Liberia." Those emigrants who were "poor and ignorant" would be allowed to vote, but their material success would depend entirely on their qualifications. For men of intelligence and means, there was no better country than Liberia; for those without means, Liberia was "one of the worst countries" to go to.[76] Most blacks in Springfield were without means.[77]

Ten years later, the Springfield black community met to discuss "the Liberia question." The Illinois Colonization Society had argued that the legislature should provide financial assistance to remove "people of color" from the state and had further asserted that "some of the most intelligent and enterprising of the people of color in the State of Illinois, desire the assistance of the Colonization Society, to enable them to remove to Liberia or some other part of Africa." The black residents named a committee to prepare resolutions. The committee declared that it had not been able to find "any intelligent man of color" who wanted to go to Africa or needed money to do so. Moreover, public expenditures for colonization would not bestow any benefit to the state or to "colored people particularly." But colonization would mean the removal of thousands of laborers. The committee observed, "The State needs laborers to cultivate the fields and to perform various other services, and we are both ready and willing to work. We also believe that the colored people of this State are, in general, as industrious and inoffensive a population as can anywhere be found." The Colonization Society's efforts would only make life worse for black residents of Illinois. The racist beliefs underlying colonization would manage to "excite prejudices against us, and to impel ignorant or ill disposed persons to take measures against us for our expulsion from the land of our nativity."[78]

The resolutions ended with a claim to "the rights of citizenship in this, the country of our birth." The black residents of Springfield rejected colonization because "we were born here, and here we desire to die and to be buried." They were not "aliens either in blood or in race, to the people of the country in which we were born." They then asked, "Why then should we be disenfranchised and denied the rights of citizenship in the north, and those of human nature itself in the south?"[79]

In 1853 African Americans held a statewide convention in Chicago.[80] The delegates passed several resolutions; the first three strongly condemned colonization. All schemes for colonization were "directly calculated to increase pro-slavery prejudice, to depress our moral energies, to unsettle all our plans for improvement, and finally to perpetuate the wicked and horrible system of slavery."[81] Five years later, black Chicagoans met at the African Methodist Episcopal church to discuss emigration from the United States. H. Ford Douglas proposed that the "colored citizens" of Chicago would no longer submit to "the oppression of the Saxon" and that emigrating to some other spot on the continent (Douglas favored Canada) would end slavery and bring about "the elevation of our race." Douglas's resolutions were defeated, receiving but one vote. Resolutions condemning emigration were proposed and adopted instead. The resolutions rejected the notion that nature had set aside any place on earth for the exclusive benefit of any one class, as "all men have a natural right to live where it may seem best to them." This talk of emigration would only revive "the old Colonization scheme, against which we have long since protested." They ended with a firm declaration that the colored citizens of Chicago were not going anywhere: "as we have been with this people from the beginning, we intend to remain with them until the end; we have planted our trees in the American Soil, and by the help of God, we mean to repose under the shade thereof."[82]

Colonization had been popular among whites in Sangamon County early on. Springfield newspapers had expressed interest in colonization as early as 1832, when articles in the *Sangamo Journal* welcomed an interest in the American Colonization Society among white Illinoisans.[83] Three different county-level colonization societies were formed between 1833 and 1846. The first such attempt was the Springfield, Sangamon County Colonization Society, which was established in August 1833. Its eleven officers included Charles R. Matheny and John T. Stuart. Lincoln, who was then living in New Salem, was not an officer in the society.[84] This attempt must have been short-lived because another county-level colonization society, the Sangamon Colonization Society, was established in 1839. This colonization society began with a flourish—its first annual meeting enlisted 150 members and raised $350 in dues to be used to "transport and settle in Africa twelve emancipated slaves." It was associated with the American Colonization Society. At its first meeting, the Reverend J. T. Mitchell proposed that "the cause of *African Colonization* is worthy of the entire confidence, and active, unwearied support of the *American Patriot*, the *Philanthropist*, and the *Christian*." For its first year, seventeen officers were listed in the *Sangamo Journal*. Stuart was one of the five vice-presidents; his law partner, Lincoln, however, was not one of the officers.[85] This society too faded from the scene. In 1846, the year after a statewide colonization society was formed, a third county-level colonization society was established in Springfield. In its first year, this society selected sixteen officers, including Stuart and James C. Conkling. Lincoln again was missing.[86]

Lincoln was by no means a leader of the colonization movement in Illinois.[87] It is highly likely that Lincoln first supported colonization in the 1830s and 1840s, as colonization was an integral part of Whig ideology.[88] He may have argued in favor of colonization at the New Salem Literary and Debating Society.[89] But Lincoln the Whig lawyer was nowhere to be found in these early attempts to form colonization societies at a time when most officers of the Springfield colonization societies were Whig lawyers.[90] Lincoln's absence from the colonization societies of the late 1830s and 1840s is somewhat puzzling. Perhaps the simplest explanation is that Lincoln, as Allen C. Guelzo has noted, "showed little enthusiasm for entering into the broad variety of community-based societies and activities that the Illinois capital afforded."[91]

In the 1840s, pro-colonization sentiment grew in the Midwest and West.[92] The Illinois State Colonization Society, formed in Springfield in 1845, persisted throughout the 1850s.[93] In its inaugural year, the statewide society selected thirty-two officers, including sixteen vice-presidents and thirteen managers. Prominent Whig lawyers Orville H. Browning, William Brown, and James C. Conkling were among the thirty-two officers; their fellow Whig lawyer, Abraham Lincoln, was not. The following year, the state society reported the names of thirty-one officers. Again, Lincoln was not among them.[94]

The state society prepared a circular in 1850 that explained its purpose. Marked distinctions would always separate "the white and colored races." Black people could never expect to possess "the same privileges or enjoy them in the same degree, as may be the lot of the more favored citizens of this country." Although superior, whites should be sympathetic to the plight of blacks. Abolitionists would never achieve the success that the colonization movement had already achieved in restoring "temporal and moral freedom" to blacks sent to colonies in Africa. Moreover, colonization would result in "the conversion and the civilization of the continent of Africa."[95]

Lincoln would not appear before the state colonization society until 1853. The invitation to speak came the year after Lincoln first publicly addressed colonization in his eulogy for Henry Clay.[96] He was scheduled to speak at the state society's annual meeting the following year but canceled because of illness in his family.[97] In 1855 Lincoln again addressed the society. Only the outline for his speech has survived—it primarily lists important dates in the history of slavery, and antislavery, in America. The last date noted is 1816, when the American Colonization Society was organized. Lincoln discussed the American Colonization Society's history and "present prospects for success." He also discussed its direct object (colonization) and its collateral objects ("suppression of slave trade—commerce—civilization and religion"). The Springfield correspondent for a St. Louis newspaper briefly reported that Lincoln, who was running for the US Senate at the time, was "emphatically non-committal." Lincoln supported "the project of colonizing" only if it "could be accomplished without trouble, without confusion."[98] It is not clear what Lincoln meant by trouble or confusion. Lincoln apparently did not give much significance to his two addresses to the state colonization society. He did not think either speech was important enough to arrange for its publication, which is something he did for other speeches in this period.[99] The Whig paper did not even bother to provide a report on either speech. The soporific outline that survives for the 1855 speech suggests why.

Twenty years after moving to Springfield, Lincoln became an officer of one of the city's colonization societies. In 1857 Lincoln was selected as one of the eleven managers of the state colonization society. The following year, he was reappointed a manager. Since the Illinois State Colonization Society does not seem to have accomplished much, these appointments as manager appear to be honorific posts. In 1856 Lincoln became a dues-paying member of the American Colonization Society. Unlike Stephen Douglas, who was listed for seven consecutive years (1854–1860) as one of the many vice-presidents of the American Colonization Society, Lincoln never held office in it.[100]

Lincoln on Colonization

In the 1850s Lincoln made a handful of speeches addressing colonization. He first mentioned it during his eulogy for Henry Clay in 1852. He discussed Clay's advocacy of colonization as part of his antislavery principles. Clay favored gradual emancipation of the slaves in Kentucky because Clay "did not perceive, that on a question of human right, the negroes were to be exempted from the human race." Clay was not an abolitionist because slavery could not be "at once eradicated, without producing a greater evil, even to the cause of human liberty itself." Clay, like Lincoln, opposed "both extremes of opinions" on slavery. Clay opposed abolitionists "who would shiver into fragments the Union of these States; tear to tatters its now venerated constitution; and even burn the last copy of the Bible, rather than slavery should continue a single hour." Clay also opposed the proslavery ideologues who would "assail and ridicule the white man's charter of freedom—the declaration that 'all men are created equal.'"[101]

Avoiding both extremes, Clay chose colonization as a middle ground. Lincoln quoted Clay's 1827 speech before the American Colonization Society.[102] He then praised Clay's association with the society as one of its earliest members; Clay was also president of the American Colonization Society, giving the society its "very greatest collateral support." Clay did not believe it was a "demerit" to the society "that it tended to relieve slave-holders from the troublesome presence of the free negroes" because this was far from being its "whole merit."[103]

Lincoln repeated Clay's claim that there was a "moral fitness" in returning to Africa "her children, whose ancestors have been torn from here by the ruthless hand of fraud and violence." Like most exponents of colonization, neither Clay nor Lincoln paused to question whether black people born in America were still children of Africa or whether freed blacks would want to return. Lincoln repeated an additional argument made by Clay: repatriated blacks would carry with them the "rich fruits of religion, civilization, law and liberty." Lincoln asserted that the valuable lessons learned as slaves could possibly result in the "ultimate redemption of the African race and African continent." The "friends of colonization," Lincoln said, hoped our countrymen would "succeed in freeing our land from the dangerous presence of slavery, and, at the same time, in restoring a captive people to their long-lost father-land, with bright prospects for the future; and this too, so gradually, that neither races nor individuals shall have suffered by the change."[104] These were all standard American Colonization Society themes, stressing the benevolence of colonization.[105]

Lincoln returned to the topic of colonization in his Springfield speech on the *Dred Scott* decision in June 1857. Lincoln noted that he had said before that "the separation of the races is the only perfect preventive of amalgamation." While the Republican Party platform did not call for such separation, most Republicans were for it, and "the chief plank in their platform—opposition to the spread of slavery—is most favorable to that separation." Separation "if ever effected at all, must be effected by colonization." But no political party was "doing anything directly for colonization." Colonization would be a "difficult enterprise," but what it needed most was a "hearty will." The will for colonization would spring from both "moral sense and self-interest." It was morally right and "favorable to, or at least, not against, our interest, to transfer the African to his native clime." Only the Republican Party could create the "public sentiment" for colonization because only the Republican Party held that "the negro is a man" and "his bondage is cruelly wrong." The Democrats denied "his manhood" and "deny, or dwarf to insignificance, the wrong of his bondage."[106]

Colonization was barely discussed during the US Senate race the following year. In his opening speech of the Senate campaign, Lincoln said what he would "most desire would be the separation of the white and black races" after declaring black people were entitled to their natural rights.[107] In two other speeches, Lincoln mentioned colonization when he was assuming the mantle of Henry Clay. In Edwardsville, Illinois, Lincoln described Clay as an "earnest advocate of a system of gradual emancipation and colonization."[108] In the last debate with Douglas, Lincoln argued that he was an "old line Whig" whose views on slavery were no different from those of Henry Clay. He quoted Clay several times and included a line from a speech where Clay said, "I wish every slave in the United States was in the country of his ancestors."[109] Those were the only instances where Lincoln mentioned colonization during the Senate campaign.

One Illinois Republican wrote Lincoln to urge that the state convention consider adopting a resolution supporting colonization, but no such resolution was considered.[110] The Illinois Republican Party platform did not mention colonization.[111] When Republican newspapers ran side-by-side comparisons of Lincoln and Clay, they included quotations showing that both favored the "separation of races."[112] While some Republican newspapers asserted that colonization was part of the "Republican creed," such mentions of colonization appear to be rare.[113] In 1860, after several state Republican Party conventions adopted pro-colonization planks in their platforms, both supporters and opponents of colonization expected a pro-colonization plank in the Republican Party's national platform; however, the platform did not mention colonization, and Lincoln's support for colonization was not mentioned by his proxies.[114]

In the fall of 1860, the Haitian government organized an effort to encourage immigration to Haiti "among the colored American population." One objective of this campaign was gaining US diplomatic recognition of Haiti. Richard J. Hinton toured the North as a special agent of the Haitian government. In December Hinton discussed diplomatic recognition with the president-elect in Springfield.

Lincoln wanted to avoid any "public discussion" of the topic, while conceding that the issue "would ultimately be raised and must be met." (The Lincoln administration recognized Haiti in 1862.) Hinton found Lincoln "decidedly in favor of a separation of races" provided that, in Lincoln's words, "it could be brought about fairly and voluntarily."[115] Lincoln soon would have an opportunity to bring about such colonization projects.

Lincoln supported the Black Laws of Illinois, even refusing to join other Republicans in calling for repeal of the testimony law that prohibited blacks from testifying in court. While not an active leader in the colonization movement, he publicly supported black emigration in several speeches in the 1850s. Lincoln barely mentioned colonization in the Senate race in 1858, and the Republican Party did not include colonization in its 1860 platform, which made his active support for colonization in the first two years of his administration more surprising.

This lithograph by H. Bucholzer depicts a nativist riot in Philadelphia in 1844. Lincoln and his fellow Whigs in Springfield met to refute charges by Democrats that Whigs were hostile to foreigners and Catholics. Library of Congress.

In this 1854 daguerreotype taken in Chicago by Polycarpus von Schneidau, Lincoln was holding a German-language newspaper. Library of Congress.

This 1854 lithograph, *Uncle Sam's Youngest Son, Citizen Know Nothing*, portrays the idealized nativist male. Lincoln wanted to bring Know-Nothings into the anti-Nebraska movement while rejecting "Know-Nothingism." Library of Congress.

These portraits of Dred and Harriet Scott were published in *Century* magazine in 1887, thirty years after Chief Justice Roger B. Taney held that a free black man had "no rights which the white man was bound to respect." The issue of black citizenship figured prominently in the 1858 Lincoln-Douglas debates. Library of Congress.

This carte de visite of Frederick Douglass was taken by Edwin Burke Ives and Reuben L. Andrews three weeks after Lincoln issued the Emancipation Proclamation. Douglass believed that Lincoln, during the course of the Civil War, "came to look upon the Black man as an American citizen." Hillsdale College.

African American artist David Bustill Bowser created eleven battle flags for black regiments. The battle flag of the Twenty-Fourth Regiment of United States Colored Troops implores, “Let Soldiers in War, Be Citizens in Peace.” Library of Congress.

The battle flag of the 127th Regiment of United States Colored Troops, also created by Bowser, expresses one of the goals of black military service: "We Will Prove Ourselves Men." Photo courtesy of Morphy Auctions, morphyauctions.com.

This 1863 Currier and Ives lithograph portrays "the gallant charge of the Fifty Fourth Massachusetts (Colored) Regiment" at Fort Wagner. The racial attitudes of northern whites, including Lincoln, changed because of the bravery and sacrifice of black soldiers. Library of Congress.

CHAPTER FOUR

DRED SCOTT AND BLACK CITIZENSHIP

The *Dred Scott* decision ensured that black citizenship would become one of the dominant themes of the 1858 Illinois race for the US Senate. In his debates with Stephen A. Douglas, Abraham Lincoln would reiterate his opposition to black citizenship, while Douglas repeatedly tried to portray Lincoln and the Republican Party as advocates of political and social equality for the black race.

"No Rights Which the White Man Was Bound to Respect"

After losing a freedom lawsuit in state court, Dred Scott sued his ostensible owner, John A. Sandford, in federal district court in 1854. Since federal courts have limited jurisdiction, Scott had to establish that the federal court had jurisdiction over his lawsuit. The Constitution affords jurisdiction to "controversies . . . between citizens of different states." Scott's lawyers asserted that his lawsuit belonged in federal court because he was a citizen of Missouri and Sandford was a citizen of New York. Sandford's lawyers responded by filing a plea in abatement, objecting to the basis of jurisdiction. They argued that Scott could not claim to be a citizen because he was "a negro of African descent, whose ancestors were of pure African blood, and who were brought into the country and sold as slaves."[1] After losing the trial in the district court, Scott appealed to the US Supreme Court.

The Supreme Court announced its decision on March 6, 1857. Chief Justice Roger B. Taney posed two major issues in his opinion. First, could Dred Scott be considered a citizen entitled to sue in federal court? Second, did Congress have the power to prohibit slavery in the territories? Taney ruled that no black person could be considered a citizen and that Congress lacked the power to prohibit slavery in the territories.

Taney held that Dred Scott could not be a citizen simply because he was black. Descendants of slaves could not be considered members of the "political community." They were not "included, and were not intended to be included under the word 'citizens' in the Constitution." They were instead considered to be "a subordinate and inferior class of beings, who had been subjugated by the dominant race."[2] Taney had to create a form of dual citizenship to achieve his purposes. While the prevailing view before *Dred Scott* was that "anyone who was considered a citizen of a state was also a citizen of the United States," Taney asserted that the "rights of citizenship which a state may confer within its own limits" could not be confounded with the "rights of citizenship as a member of the Union."[3] Black people could not be citizens of the United States. The "negro race" was a separate class of persons, "not regarded as a portion of the people or citizens of the Government then formed." Taney explained:

> They had for more than a century before been regarded as beings of an inferior order, and altogether unfit to associate with the white race, either in social or political relations; and so far inferior that they had no rights which the white man was bound to respect; and that the negro might justly and lawfully be reduced to slavery for his benefit. He was bought and sold, and treated as an ordinary article of merchandise and traffic, whenever a profit could be made by it. This opinion was at that time fixed and universal in the civilized portion of the white race.

Race became a "perpetual and impassable barrier." The "unhappy black race were separated from the white by indelible marks."[4]

Taney rejected the universal language of the Declaration of Independence. Like Stephen A. Douglas, Taney argued that the phrase "all men are created equal" meant "all white men are created equal." Taney conceded that the "general words" of the Declaration would "seem to embrace the whole human family"; nonetheless it was "too clear for dispute, that the enslaved African race were not intended to be included, and formed no part of the people who framed and adopted this declaration."[5]

Associate justices John McLean and Benjamin R. Curtis filed lengthy dissents, and both made points that are relevant here.[6] McLean pointed to the different meanings of citizenship. To be able to invoke jurisdiction in federal court as a citizen, Dred Scott did not need to possess the qualifications of an "elector." Women and minors could sue in federal courts, and they certainly were not voters. All that was necessary to be a citizen for jurisdictional purposes was to be "born under our Constitution and laws." Dred Scott was not a foreigner, so naturalization was not required to make him a citizen. McLean concluded that the "most general and appropriate definition" of *citizen* was "a freeman." Since Dred Scott was a freeman with "his domicile in a state different from that of the defendant, he is a citizen." McLean also pointed out the historical errors in Taney's opinion. Taney overlooked how "several of the States have admitted persons of color to the right of suffrage, and in this view have recognised them as citizens."[7]

Curtis's dissent addressed the issue of citizenship at great length. Sandford's plea in abatement alleged that Dred Scott was not a citizen of Missouri "because he is a negro of African descent; his ancestors were of pure African blood, and were brought into this country and sold as negro slaves." The question became whether any person of African descent can be a citizen of the United States: "If any such person can be a citizen, this plaintiff has the right to the judgment of the court that he is so."[8]

Curtis used the historical record to show that black residents were citizens of states under the Articles of Confederation at the time of the adoption of the Constitution: "Of this there can be no doubt." He established that free black people in New Hampshire, Massachusetts, New York, New Jersey, and North Carolina "were not only citizens of those States, but such of them as had the other necessary qualifications possessed the franchise of electors, on equal terms with other citizens." The Articles of Confederation also posited that "the free inhabitants of each of these states" shall be entitled to "all the privileges and immunities of free citizens in the several States." South Carolina attempted to amend that provision by inserting the word *white* between "free" and "inhabitants" so that "the privileges and immunities of general citizenship would be secured only to white persons." Eight states voted against the amendment, two were in favor, and one state's vote was divided. It was clear, argued Curtis, that when the Constitution was adopted, "free colored persons of African descent might be, and, by reason of their citizenship in certain States, were entitled to the privileges and immunities of general citizenship of the United States." The Constitution did not deprive them of citizenship. Black people were not only included in the body of "the people of the United States," but in at least five states they were able to vote on the ratification of the Constitution.

Curtis also addressed the relationship of suffrage to citizenship. While the "enjoyment of the elective franchise" was not essential to citizenship, there was no doubt that "it is one of the chiefest attributes of citizenship under the American Constitutions; and the just and constitutional possession of this right is decisive evidence of citizenship." But each state decided who was entitled to the vote: "One may confine the right of suffrage to white male citizens; another may extend it to colored persons and females." (Eleven years after the convention in Seneca Falls, women's suffrage was considered within the range of civic possibility.) And in five of the original thirteen states, black men could vote.[9]

The white republic envisioned by Taney was assailed by Curtis. The Constitution, he pointed out, was not "made exclusively by and for the white race." The very preamble of the Constitution declared that "it was ordained and established by the people of the United States, for themselves and their posterity," contradicting the notion that it was created only for whites.[10]

Lincoln and Douglas Set the Stage

The North had a variety of reactions to *Dred Scott*.[11] The free black community was appalled and disgusted by Taney's pronouncements on black citizenship. Frederick Douglass decried "this devilish decision—

this judicial incarnation of wolfishness."[12] White abolitionists also criticized this portion of Taney's opinion, but such voices were in the minority. Taney's denial of black citizenship "carried nothing like the same emotional charge as his ruling against the Missouri Compromise restriction."[13] Republicans, who wanted to stop the expansion of slavery into the territories, directed most of their attacks on Taney's ruling about the constitutionality of the Missouri Compromise. After all, free soil and free labor formed "the lowest common denominator of Republican appeal."[14]

In June 1857, both Stephen A. Douglas and Lincoln gave speeches primarily focused on *Dred Scott.* Douglas's speech came first, and Lincoln intended his remarks—delivered two weeks later—to be an "answer" to Douglas's.[15] Douglas emphasized Taney's holding on black citizenship, which he called the "main proposition decided by the court." Douglas wanted to portray all Republicans as egalitarians and abolitionists. The "Republican or Abolition party" believed that the Declaration of Independence was intended to include "negroes, as well as white men; that it embraced men of all races and colors, and placed them on a footing of entire and absolute equality."[16]

If this Republican belief in "the perfect equality of all races" prevailed in Illinois, Douglas warned, it would change the constitution and laws of Illinois. The constitutional provision that denied black people "the right to come and live among us" would have to be struck down. Black men would be able to vote "on an equality with white men—and of course, outvote us at the polls when they become a majority." They would also be eligible for office, including the presidency. Black citizenship would inevitably result in the repeal of "all laws making any distinction whatever on account of race and color, and authorize negroes to marry white women on an equality with white men."[17] Douglas warned that political equality would lead to demands for social equality: "But when you confer upon the African race the privileges of citizenship, and put them upon an equality with white men at the polls, in the jury box, on the bench, in the executive chair, and in the councils of the nation, upon what principle will you deny their equality at the festive board and in the domestic circle." The Supreme Court had averted this supposed nightmare, Douglas emphasized, by holding "under the constitution, a negro is not and cannot be a citizen."[18]

Although the *Dred Scott* decision had been announced three months earlier, Lincoln had yet to comment on it publicly.[19] After hearing Douglas's speech, Lincoln decided it was time to respond. He spent the next two weeks in the library of the Illinois Supreme Court reading the *Dred Scott* opinions and commentaries on the case. On the evening of June 26, Lincoln arrived at the Illinois House of Representatives prepared and carrying his law books.[20]

Lincoln, like Douglas, largely focused on Taney's holding on citizenship. Like other Republicans, Lincoln's response to Taney's ruling on the unconstitutionality of the Missouri Compromise, which essentially destroyed the ability of Republicans to keep slavery out of the territories, was limited to attacking its strength as precedent and asserting that it failed to establish "a settled doctrine for the country."[21]

Lincoln spent much more time addressing the ruling on citizenship, which was somewhat surprising for a politician in a state that failed to recognize its black residents held any citizenship rights. Lincoln made four points: (1) Taney was wrong on the historical facts concerning black citizenship during the founding era, (2) the Declaration of Independence's axiom that "all men are created equal" applied to black people, (3) "amalgamation" was a great evil to be avoided, and (4) colonization presented the best solution to the problem of race in America.[22]

Lincoln attacked Taney's opinion because it was, "in part, based on assumed historical facts which are not really true." The part that was not really true was Taney's insistence that black people were not "part of the people who made, or for whom was made, the Declaration of Independence, or the Constitution of the United States."[23] Lincoln relied on and quoted from Curtis's dissenting opinion to establish that in five of the original thirteen states, free blacks were voters and had the "same part in making the Constitution that the white people had."[24]

Lincoln also criticized Taney's implicit assumption that "the public estimate of the black man is more favorable *now* than it was in the days of the Revolution." This was obviously false: the "change between then and now is decidedly the other way." The "ultimate destiny" for black people in America "has never appeared so hopeless as in the last three or four years." Of the five states that allowed black suffrage, two had taken that right away. Lincoln now lamented how the right to vote for free blacks had been "greatly abridged" in New York, a state that figured prominently in Lincoln's race-baiting attacks on Van Buren more than two decades earlier. No state had extended the right to vote to blacks even though the number of states had doubled.

Why did Lincoln spend so much of his speech on Taney's holding on citizenship? As a lawyer, he could not help himself. When Lincoln prepared for his response to Douglas's speech, he "examined that decision with a good deal of care, as a lawyer examines a decision."[25] And when lawyer Lincoln examined *Dred Scott*, he was "at the head of his profession in his state" and at the height of his legal prowess.[26] He had become a particularly skilled appellate lawyer, adept at legal reasoning and deep analysis of texts.[27] In the two preceding years, Lincoln had handled more than forty appellate cases in the Illinois Supreme Court.[28]

Lincoln's experience and expertise made dissecting Taney's holding on citizenship too easy a target.[29] Douglas lambasted Republicans for believing "all men are created equal," and Lincoln did not deny this charge. Instead he lamented how the plain meaning of the Declaration—once "held sacred by all, and thought to include all"—was "assailed, and sneered at, and construed, and hawked at, and torn."[30] The Declaration of Independence set up a "standard maxim for free society": that all men are created equal. This did not mean, as Douglas charged, that all men were equal "*in all respects.*" Men were not equal "in color, size, intellect, moral development, or social capacity." They were equal "in certain inalienable rights, among which are life, liberty, and the pursuit of happiness." In a point repeated in his debates with Douglas the following year, Lincoln assailed the "counterfeit logic" maintaining that, because he did not want a black woman for a slave, he must want her for a wife. Instead, said Lincoln, he "can just leave her alone." While "in some respects she certainly is not my equal; but in her natural right to eat the bread she earns with her own hands without asking leave of anyone else, she is my equal, and the equal of all others."[31]

Earlier in the year, after the city elections in Chicago where Republicans fared poorly, Lincoln had complained, "We were constantly charged with seeking an amalgamation of the white and black races; and thousands turned from us."[32] Douglas continued this effective attack on Republicans in his June speech. Lincoln's response: nearly all white people are disgusted by the idea of "an indiscriminate amalgamation of the white and black races; and Judge Douglas evidently is basing his chief hope, upon the chances of being able to appropriate the benefit of this disgust to himself." Douglas wants voters to believe that Republicans "want to vote, and eat, and sleep, and marry with negroes." After noting Douglas's horror at the thought of whites and blacks "mixing blood," Lincoln responded, "agreed for once—a thousand times agreed."[33]

When the campaign in Illinois for the US Senate began in the summer of 1858, Douglas returned to his attack on Lincoln's support for black citizenship. On July 9, 1858—a month before the debates between Lincoln and Douglas began—Douglas critiqued Lincoln's House Divided speech at the Republican state convention. Douglas charged that Lincoln's real objection to *Dred Scott* was its declaration that "a negro, descended from African parents," could not be a citizen of the United States. Lincoln thought that was wrong because "it deprives the negro of the benefits" of the privilege and immunities clause of the Constitution. Douglas's rejoinder: "this government of ours is founded on the white basis. It was made by the white man, for the benefit of the white man, to be administered by the white man, in such manner as they should determine." A member of an inferior race could be afforded such "rights, privileges, and immunities which he is capable of exercising consistent with the safety of society," yet this was a decision each state must make for itself. Illinois had decided that "the negro shall not be a slave"—and that "he shall not vote, or serve on juries, or enjoy political privileges."[34]

Although Douglas's July speech had attacked Lincoln over his purported support for black citizenship, Lincoln failed to discuss Taney's holding on citizenship again until the debates began later that summer. Lincoln gave at least eight speeches after Douglas's July speech and before the first debate in Ottawa on August 21.[35] He often mentioned *Dred Scott*, and he just as often disclaimed any support for black political or social equality.

Except for Taney's holding on citizenship, Lincoln returned to all the other arguments he had raised in his address on *Dred Scott* the previous year. While he believed black people were entitled to their natural rights of "life, liberty, and the pursuit of happiness," Lincoln had no "disposition to make negroes perfectly equal with white men in social and political relations."[36] He rejected Douglas's "repeated charges" that Republicans had an "inclination to marry with and hug negroes."[37] Lincoln continued to discuss the distinction between natural rights and social and political ones. He eloquently praised the founders for their "majestic interpretation of the economy of the Universe." Natural rights belonged to "the whole great family of man." These "great self-evident truths" established in the Declaration of Independence were intended to prevent anyone in the "distant future" from setting up a contrary doctrine that "none but rich men, or none but white men" were entitled to these rights.[38] Lincoln did not desire "*negro equality* in all things, *he only wanted that the words* of the Declaration of Independence should be applied" to all those to whom it was meant to be applied.[39]

Lincoln's specific remarks on *Dred Scott* in these speeches were directed at its limitations as a precedent. Lincoln returned to his view on the two different functions of judicial opinions: a court both settled the dispute between the parties brought before it, and it proclaimed rules to resolve future disputes of a similar kind. Lincoln explained that he offered no resistance to the court's finding that Dred Scott was a slave. He did refuse, however, to follow the court's decision as a political rule.[40]

The Lincoln-Douglas Debates

The debates between Lincoln and Douglas began in Ottawa, Illinois, on August 21, 1858. In Douglas's opening speech, the first of twenty-one speeches in the seven debates, Douglas tied Lincoln's opposition to *Dred Scott* to Lincoln's support for black citizenship. Lincoln opposed *Dred Scott* because "he says it deprives the negro of the rights and privileges of citizenship." That was Lincoln's "first and main reason" for his "warfare on the Supreme Court." Douglas asked his audience a series of rhetorical questions, including whether they wanted to strike from the 1848 Illinois Constitution the "clause which keeps slaves and free negroes out of the state, and allow the free negroes to flow in, and cover your prairies with black settlements?"[41] According to Douglas, the audience faced a stark choice between Douglas and the Democratic Party and Lincoln and the "Black Republicans." If they wanted citizenship for black people, they should vote for Lincoln, who was no better than "all the little abolition orators" who claimed the Declaration of Independence proclaims equality between whites and blacks. Douglas did not question Lincoln's "belief that the negro was made his equal, and hence is his brother."[42] After the first hour of the first debate, Douglas had Lincoln on the defensive.

Lincoln did not directly respond to Douglas's claim that he opposed *Dred Scott* because of Taney's stance on black citizenship. He instead reaffirmed his opposition to black political equality. He used his 1854 speech on the Kansas-Nebraska Act to establish that he had not engaged in "abolitionizing the old Whig party." Lincoln's point in 1854 was the same point he wanted to make in 1858: not knowing what to do about slavery where it already existed did not provide any excuse for permitting its territorial extension.[43]

Lincoln then reiterated his opposition to any "perfect social and political equality with the negro." He twice used the N-word as if to prove he was just as racist as Douglas, denying that he had a "tendency" to set "the niggers and white people marrying together."[44] There was no difference between Douglas and him on whites holding the "superior position" in society: "I have no purpose to introduce political and social equality between the white and the black races. There is a physical difference between the two, which in my judgment will probably forever forbid their living together upon the footing of perfect equality, and inasmuch as it becomes a necessity that there must be a difference, I, as well as Judge Douglas, am in favor of the race to which I belong, having the superior position." Nonetheless, blacks would still be entitled to "all the natural rights enumerated in the Declaration of Independence—the right to life, liberty, and the pursuit of happiness."[45]

The next extended skirmish on black citizenship was at Charleston, in the fourth debate, which was held on September 18. Lincoln gave the opening speech and began his remarks by mentioning an "elderly gentleman" who had asked him at the hotel earlier whether he was "really in favor of producing a perfect equality between the negroes and white people." Lincoln then gave his infamous paean to white supremacy:

> I will say that I am not, nor ever have been, in favor of bringing about in any way the social and political equality of the white and black races; that I am not, nor ever have been, in favor of making voters or jurors of negroes, nor of qualifying them to hold office, nor to intermarry with white people. And I will say in addition to this that there is a physical difference between the white and black races which I believe will forever forbid the two races living together on terms of social and political equality. And inasmuch as they cannot so live, while they do remain together there must be the position of superior and inferior, and I as much as any other man am in favor of having the superior position assigned to the white race.

Because the white man was to have the superior position did not mean "the negro should be denied everything."[46]

Lincoln proclaimed that he had never met anyone "who was in favor of producing a perfect equality, social and political, between negroes and white men." The only instance that Lincoln could recall of such "perfect equality" was "the case of Judge Douglas's old friend, Col. Richard M. Johnson." Lincoln joked that he had never suffered "the least apprehension" that he or his friends would marry black women if there were no laws against it, yet Douglas and his friends seem to be in "great apprehension" that they might do so unless interracial marriages remained prohibited. He jokingly assured Douglas that he would, "to the very last, stand by the law of his state which forbids the marrying of white people with negroes."[47]

Douglas countered Lincoln's disclaimer of black equality with two responses. First, Douglas indirectly responded by claiming that Republicans had "colored gentlemen for their advocates." In 1854 Lincoln and Lyman Trumbull had joined an alliance with "Lincoln's ally," abolitionist "Fred Douglass, the negro," against the Democratic Party. Then, the Republicans "had the same negro hunting me down," and now the Republicans again had "a negro traversing the Northern counties of the state, and speaking in behalf of Lincoln." In fact, Douglas maintained, "a distinguished colored friend" of Lincoln's was on the stump for him at Freeport, Illinois. This showed how much interest "the colored brethren felt in the success of their brother Abe."[48]

Douglas's second response was to demand that Lincoln state his position: "I want to know whether he is for or against negro citizenship?" Douglas returned to Lincoln's House Divided speech, where, according to Douglas, Lincoln declared his opposition to *Dred Scott* because the Supreme Court had decided "that it was not possible for a negro to be a citizen under the Constitution of the United States." If Lincoln disagreed with the court on that point, then he "must be in favor of conferring the right and privilege of citizenship upon the negro!"[49]

When Lincoln began his rejoinder, he immediately turned to Douglas's question: "I tell him very frankly that I am not in favor of negro citizenship." Fortunately for Lincoln, Douglas referenced the House Divided speech from June and not the speech on *Dred Scott* from 1857. Lincoln could plausibly explain that the reference to citizenship in the 1858 speech was restating "one of the points decided in the course of the Supreme Court opinions." Lincoln said he had not expressed any objection to that holding, which was not true, as he did object to it in 1857. Lincoln said his opinion was that "the different states have the power to make a negro a citizen under the Constitution," but *Dred Scott* had decided that states do not have that power. If Illinois still had that power, Lincoln said he would be opposed to its exercise.[50]

Douglas certainly thought Lincoln could not logically maintain a position holding that blacks were entitled to the natural rights declared in the Declaration of Independence while also holding that blacks belonged to an inferior race. He began his rejoinder at Galesburg with that very point. He accused Lincoln of backtracking from his stance on black inferiority that he had expressed at the previous debate.[51]

Douglas's charge that Lincoln's position on black citizenship changed depending on where he was in the state was having an impact. In Lincoln's opening speech at the next debate in Quincy, he addressed the accusation of "double-dealing with the public." Lincoln pointed out that at the first debate in Ottawa, he had quoted his 1854 speech to show that his sentiments on black equality were "long entertained and openly expressed." Lincoln consistently had argued that black people were entitled to natural rights, but "a social and political equality between the white and black races" was an "utter impossibility."[52]

At the last debate, held in Alton, Douglas gave the opening speech. Douglas again returned to Lincoln's House Divided speech to attack Lincoln on black citizenship. Lincoln's "crusade" against the Supreme Court because of *Dred Scott* was based upon an "especial reason"—the opinion "deprived the negroes of the rights and benefits" of citizenship. Lincoln and the Republican Party detested *Dred Scott* because it denied blacks equality with whites. Douglas once again trumpeted the cause of white supremacy. The founders did not intend the phrase "all men are created equally" to apply equally to all men: "They did not mean negro, nor the savage Indians, nor the Fejee [Fiji] Islanders, nor any other barbarous race."[53]

Lincoln responded by stating, plausibly, that he had not "in a very especial manner complained that the Supreme Court in the Dred Scott case had decided that a negro could never be a citizen of the United States." Lincoln tried to explain that he had merely stated the court's decision as part of a larger argument about a scheme to make slavery national. He only "mentioned as a fact that they had decided that a negro could not be a citizen." He supposed that the court had wanted to deprive the negro "under all circumstances, of the remotest possibility of ever becoming a citizen." But, Lincoln claimed, he was not "making any complaint of it at all."[54]

Lincoln more broadly claimed that he had not complained "*especially* of the Dred Scott decision because it held a negro could not be a citizen, and the Judge is always wrong when he says I ever did so complain of it." After making this broader claim, Lincoln immediately returned to his House Divided speech. The broader claim would be difficult for Lincoln to sustain, since his 1857 speech on *Dred Scott* did complain *especially* of the holding on black citizenship and did not merely restate what the court—or, more accurately, Taney—had written on black citizenship. It is a mystery why Douglas used the House Divided speech as the only evidence that Lincoln supported black citizenship.[55]

Democrats tried to depict Lincoln as an abolitionist, and they particularly liked to link Lincoln with Frederick Douglass.[56] Douglas mentioned Douglass—whom he called "Fred. Douglass" or "Fred. Douglass, the negro"—at five of the seven debates.[57] Twice he told a story about seeing Douglass sitting in a carriage with a white woman, thus painting an image calculated to horrify his audience: "a beautiful young lady . . . sitting on the box seat, whilst Fred Douglass and her mother reclined inside, and the owner of the carriage acted as driver."[58] At Jonesboro, Douglas said the Republicans "brought out men to canvass the state whose complexion suited their political creed."[59] For his part, Douglass, in a speech in New York, had called "all the friends of negro equality and negro citizenship" to rally around Lincoln to defeat Douglas.[60]

Throughout the Senate campaign, Lincoln's fellow Republicans warned him about the perils of black equality. Lyman Trumbull, elected senator in 1855, cautioned Lincoln in June: "It will not do, of course to get mixed up with the free negro question."[61] John M. Palmer asked Lincoln to come to Macoupin County to prevent former Know-Nothing voters from "joining the Douglassites" because "Negro Equality goes hard with some Americans."[62] David Davis warned that among "the Kentuckians" it was "industriously circulated that, *you favor negro* equality." All campaign speakers needed to "distinctly & emphatically disavow *negro suffrage*—negro holding office, serving on juries, & the like."[63] Lincoln's disavowal of black citizenship during the debates had an impact, according to Owen

Lovejoy. He believed that "the bugaboo of Negro Equality has pretty much lost its power."[64]

Few Republicans shared Lovejoy's optimistic viewpoint, and several urged Lincoln to continue making the point. When Jediah F. Alexander asked Lincoln to visit Bond County in August, he advised Lincoln to be "full and explicit in explaining" that "the Republicans are not in favor of making the Blacks socially and politically equal with the Whites." Some folks in Bond County "are so hard of understanding, and like to hear a good thing repeated."[65] Before the debate at Freeport on August 27, Joseph Medill counseled Lincoln to make something clear, namely, any claims that Lincoln and other Republicans thought black people equal to whites were "*humbug, slang* and trash, uttered to deceive the ignorant and *swindle* foolish men out of their votes."[66]

Man in the Middle

Until April 1865, Lincoln's view on black citizenship always represented the mainstream of the Republican Party.[67] Lincoln's stance changed over the course of the Civil War, as did that of other mainstream Republicans. His view on black labor subtly changed before the war came. Lincoln discussed white labor and black labor differently. Like most Republicans, Lincoln "looked down upon those who labored for wages all their lives."[68] Lincoln rejected the "mud-sill theory" that a hired laborer is "fatally fixed for life."[69] Lincoln believed that the American system gave every hired laborer what historian Gabor Boritt called "the right to rise."[70] The free labor system was "the just and generous, and prosperous system, which opens the way for all—gives hope to all, and energy, and progress, and improvement of condition to all."[71] Lincoln used his own life story as an illustration of a self-made man: "So while we do not propose any war upon capital, we do wish to allow the humblest man an equal chance to get rich with everybody else. When one starts poor, as most do in the race of life, free society is such that he knows he can better his condition; he knows that there is no fixed condition of labor, for his whole life. I am not ashamed to confess that twenty five years ago I was a hired laborer, mauling rails, at work on a flat-boat—just what happens to any poor man's son!"[72] If anyone continued through life as a "hired laborer, it is not the fault of the system, but because of either a dependent nature which prefers it, or improvidence, folly, or singular misfortune.'[73]

When Lincoln spoke about free black labor, he did not usually mention the opportunity for advancement that was "the true, genuine principle of free labor." It was clear that Lincoln in the 1850s could not conceive of a black laborer having the "ability to become an employer."[74] Lincoln did not extol black people's right to rise. Instead he repeatedly emphasized individuals' right to keep the results of their manual labor—the natural right to eat the bread they had earned with their own hands. He first mentioned this right in his speech on *Dred Scott* in 1857.[75] During the Senate campaign, he mentioned the natural right to enjoy the fruit of one's labor three times.[76]

In his last debate with Douglas, Lincoln complained about the "tendency to dehumanize the negro to take away the right of ever striving to be a man." This language of "striving" was like Lincoln's portrayal of immigrant laborers coming to America to "better their conditions in life," which he mentioned later in that same speech.[77] After Lincoln gave his Cooper Union speech in New York at the end of February 1860, he agreed to speak throughout New England, giving more than eleven speeches over eleven days. Most of those speeches stuck to the Cooper Union script.[78] But in speeches at Hartford and New Haven, Lincoln spoke of a shoemakers' strike in Massachusetts that had been condemned by Stephen Douglas. Lincoln said he supported the right of workers to strike.[79] In New Haven, he again praised the virtues of the free labor system. Significantly, Lincoln included black laborers when he discussed "the right to rise." He explained, "I want every man to have the chance—and I believe a black man is entitled to it—in which he *can* better his condition—when he may look forward and hope to be a hired laborer this year and the next, work for himself afterward, and finally to hire men to work for him! That is the true system."[80]

It was not surprising that Lincoln would discuss black workers' right to keep what they had earned from their labor but not discuss their opportunity to advance in a free society. Lincoln, like most whites, believed blacks were inferior to whites. Lincoln, like most whites, likely believed that the "degraded condition" of free blacks resulted from either innate inferiority or a moral defect and not from discrimination and lack of opportunity.[81] Most black families in the Midwest, of course, had to contend with an institutional racism that allowed limited prospects for financial gain.[82]

But it was somewhat surprising when Lincoln stated that a black man was entitled to a chance to better his condition. If political calculation had tempered his earlier remarks on blacks' right to their labor, that political calculation still would have applied in 1860. If blacks could better their own condition, then the arguments for colonization were weakened and the arguments for black citizenship, strengthened.

CHAPTER FIVE

CITIZENSHIP AND THE CIVIL WAR

Lincoln in the 1850s was not an abolitionist; he wanted to stop the spread of slavery in the territories and put slavery on a course to its ultimate extinction.[1] He could not foresee any circumstances where he would have to address what happens once slavery was extinct. After the Civil War became an "abolition war" and not just a war to restore the union, Lincoln had to face the same alternatives he had outlined hypothetically a decade before.[2] In 1854 he had considered three possibilities if slavery was immediately abolished—racial subordination, equal citizenship, and colonization—and had rejected all three.

But with wartime came real choices. In May 1863 the question presented to the country, according to Frederick Douglass, was "What shall be done with the Negro?" Douglass's answer: "He must not only be given freedom, but must be admitted to all the privileges of a citizen of the United States."[3] By that time Lincoln and most white northerners agreed that slaves must be given freedom, but neither Lincoln nor most whites were ready for those freed slaves to have all the privileges of citizens.

Colonization and Black Citizenship

In his first annual message to Congress in December 1861, Lincoln proposed sending out of the country those enslaved people who had become free because of the First Confiscation Act.[4] He thought some states might pass laws that would result in "persons of the same class" being "thrown upon them for disposal." He recommended Congress provide for black people who were freed by the states and "steps be taken for colonizing both classes . . . at some place, or places, in a climate congenial to them." Lincoln further suggested that "the free colored people already in the United States" be included in such colonization "so far as individuals may desire." Lincoln appeared to be advocating forced colonization of slaves suddenly freed by congressional or state action and voluntary colonization of black people who were already free.[5]

Carrying out "the plan of colonization may involve the acquiring of territory," Lincoln stated, and the appropriation of funds for territorial acquisition. If the only legitimate object of acquiring territory is to furnish homes for white men, "the emigration of colored men leaves additional room for white men remaining or coming here." Lincoln rhetorically asked with this plan of colonization, "does not the expediency amount to absolute necessity—that, without which the government itself cannot be perpetuated?"[6] His language about acquiring territory naturally raised the suspicions of Central American republics: Was Lincoln's plan for colonization part of American imperial designs?[7]

Prior to his address to Congress, Lincoln had been working on a colonization project with Ambrose W. Thompson of the Chiriquí Improvement Company that involved using free black men to excavate coal that the US Navy would purchase. His contact with Thompson may have occurred as early as May 1861. Lincoln, in an October letter to his secretary of the interior, lauded the Chiriquí project for possibly directing "negroes to some of the unoccupied lands of Central America," resulting in the "equally desirable measure to secure the removal of negroes from this country."[8]

In April 1862, Congress passed a compensated emancipation act for slaves in the District of Columbia that provided $100,000 for colonization of free black people from the District of Columbia "as may desire to emigrate to the Republics of Hayti or Liberia, or such other country beyond the limits of the United States as the President may determine."[9] Lincoln issued an unusual message to Congress about this law on the day he signed it. He noted that he had never doubted the constitutional authority of Congress to abolish slavery in the District of Columbia. (In fact, he had drafted such a law during his sole term in Congress, although his bill did not mention colonization.)[10] Lincoln also wrote he was gratified that "the two principles of compensation, and colonization, are both recognized, and practically applied in the act."[11]

This renewed interest in colonization was not universally applauded; it was abhorrent to most of the nation's black residents. A meeting of African Americans in Boston adopted several resolutions criticizing colonization that bluntly stated, "when we wish to leave the United States we can find and pay for that territory that suits us best"; "we don't want to go now," and "if anybody wants us to go they must compel us."[12]

In July 1862, the House of Representatives Select Committee on Emancipation issued a report on emancipation and colonization. The views expressed in the report paralleled Lincoln's views about colonization at that time. The committee advocated colonization largely because a major objection to emancipation came from "the opposition of a large portion of our people to the intermixture of the races, and from the association of white and black labor." The presence of a race that "cannot, and ought not to, be admitted to our social and political privileges, will be a perpetual source of injury and inquietude to both." The committee warned that the "highest interests of the white race, whether Anglo-Saxon, Celt, or Scandinavian," required that the whole country be held by the white race alone. Whether or not nature had made blacks inferior to whites, what mattered was the belief that black inferiority was "indelibly fixed" among whites. And, if blacks were denied equal rights, they would eventually try to seize those rights by "bloody revolution," which would result in their "utter annihilation or re-enslavement."[13]

The committee also somehow calculated that the labor of the four or five million black workers to be removed from the United States could be replaced by one-fifth of that number of white laborers. The natural increase of the white population and "newly stimulated immigration from Europe" would fill the gap.[14]

The races, the committee concluded, had to be separated after emancipation, and colonization was the only method available. Since whites knew that "every acre of our present domain" was intended for whites, blacks had to be removed to a home beyond the United States, to "warmer regions" where the Almighty had intended "the colored races" to live. The committee suggested Haiti, Central America, the upper portions of South America, and Liberia as "interesting fields of inquiry."[15] The same day the report was issued, Congress appropriated an additional $500,000 to enable Lincoln to colonize both the emancipated slaves in the District of Columbia and "those to be made free by the possible passage of a confiscation bill."[16] When Lincoln made his unsuccessful appeal to border states to accept compensated gradual emancipation, he stressed that land in South America for colonization "can be obtained cheaply, and in abundance." Once the numbers of freed slaves reached a critical mass, there would be sufficient number "to be company and encouragement for one another"; then "the freed people will not be so reluctant to go."[17]

Lincoln's Colonization Lecture

The following month, Lincoln addressed an African American delegation on the advantages of colonization. Members of the capital's black elite, chosen at a meeting held at Union Bethel African Methodist Episcopal Church, visited Lincoln—the first time a US president had entertained a black audience at the White House. Three of the men, including the chair of the delegation, Edward Thomas, were members of the Social, Civil, and Statistical Association, a black organization that had tried to ban emigration promoters from the capital.[18]

Lincoln was not interested in having a conversation with his guests. One historian has described the scene as Lincoln assuming the "unfortunate tone of a condescending father scolding ignorant children," while another has characterized Lincoln's language as "patronizing, unfeeling, misleading, and insulting."[19] Lincoln explained to the group that Congress had appropriated money for the colonization of "the people, or a portion of them, of African descent." It was now Lincoln's duty to favor a cause that "had for a long time been his inclination." Lincoln posed these questions: Why should the people of your race be colonized? Where should they go? And why should they leave this country? But he was not interested in hearing any answers to these questions but his own.

Lincoln explained that "without the institution of Slavery and the colored race as a basis, the war could not have an existence." If the presence of black people was responsible for the war, it was "better for us both, therefore, to be separated." Whites and blacks could not coexist in America: "You and we are different races. We have between us a broader difference than exists between almost any other two races. Whether it is right or wrong I need not discuss, but this physical difference is a great disadvantage to us both, as I think your race suffer very greatly, many of them by living among us, while ours suffer from your presence. In a word we suffer on each side."[20] (A humorist who wrote under the pseudonym Orpheus C. Kerr parodied Lincoln's tone: "Your race suffers very greatly, and our race suffers in suffering your race to suffer. In a word, we both suffer, which establishes a reason why our race should not suffer your race to remain any longer.")[21]

Lincoln sounded themes found in the early years of the American Colonization Society.[22] Slaves were suffering "the greatest wrong inflicted on any people." But even when they were free, black people would be "yet far removed from being placed on an equality with the white race." While men aspire to enjoy "equality with the best when free," not a single black man is made the equal of a white man. Lincoln told the group he was presenting this "as a fact with which we have to deal."[23]

Lincoln then made his case for colonization. While slaves would readily choose emigration over slavery, the "free colored man" is not "as much inclined to go out of the country." Lincoln said this was "an extremely selfish view of the case." Since whites were reluctant to agree to emancipation if free blacks remained in America, Lincoln suggested whites would change their minds if already-free blacks agreed to self-deport. Much could be accomplished, Lincoln asserted, if "intelligent colored men, such as are before me, would move in this manner." The success of colonization could not depend on the "very poor materials" of those enslaved at the beginning of the Civil War, "whose intellects are clouded by slavery." Lincoln stressed that it was "exceedingly important that we have men at the beginning capable of thinking as white men, and not those who have been systematically oppressed."[24]

Lincoln then turned to the other question he had posed: Where should the black people go? He mentioned Liberia but conceded that blacks might want to remain "within reach of the country of your nativity." Lincoln suggested Central America as an alternative and described the Chiriquí region and its purported "very rich coal mines."[25]

Lincoln's request to the group was somewhat anticlimactic. He asked if he could get a number of able-bodied men, with their wives and children, who would be willing to go. Lincoln, negotiating against himself, asked first for a "hundred tolerably intelligent men," then fifty, before settling on twenty-five as a "successful commencement." He asked the group to consider what he had proposed. Edward Thomas, the chair of the delegation, told Lincoln that "they would hold a consultation and in a short time give an answer." Lincoln replied, "Take your full time—no hurry at all."[26]

Two days later, Thomas wrote Lincoln to say that "we were entirely hostile to the movement until all the advantages were so ably brought to our views by you." He suggested that "leading colored men" in Philadelphia, New York, and Boston be contacted about this "movement of emigration."[27] Although Thomas used *we*, he was not representing the views of the delegation. Other members of the committee subsequently ostracized him from the Social, Civil, and Statistical Association.[28]

Two weeks after the delegation met with Lincoln, some of its members reported to a group at Union Bethel Church. The *Baltimore Sun* noted that the group did not "appear greatly to favor the President's plan of colonization" and was disappointed with the delegation exceeding its instructions.[29] That group passed a resolution that was reported in newspapers as the response to the president's proposal. It said that the "few assembled" thought it was "inexpedient, inauspicious, and impolitic to agitate the subject of emigration of the colored people of this country anywhere."[30]

Despite this disapproval, hundreds of free black people in the District of Columbia expressed interest in emigration after Lincoln appointed Senator Samuel C. Pomeroy from Kansas the agent for colonization.[31] Pomeroy published an address, "To the Free Colored People of the United States," promising "a suitable location for a great, free, and prosperous people" in Chiriquí.[32] A Republican newspaper proposed christening the new colony Linconia.[33] The Chiriquí scheme collapsed that fall because of opposition by Central American governments; not a single person emigrated there.[34] After the Chiriquí project's failure—and after the Preliminary Emancipation Proclamation was issued in September—the enthusiasm for colonization waned among the black community in the District of Columbia.[35]

Lincoln's address to the black delegation was widely published, and most African Americans received it negatively. Frederick Douglass blasted Lincoln for employing "the language and arguments of an itinerant Colonization lecturer" and displaying "all his inconsistencies, his pride of race and blood, his contempt for negroes and his canting hypocrisy." Douglass warned that Lincoln's colonization schemes furnished "a weapon to all the ignorant and base, who need only the countenance of men in authority to commit all kinds of violence and outrage upon the colored people of the country."[36] This was not an idle concern; Lincoln was blaming African Americans for the Civil War at a time of increased racial violence.[37] Robert Purvis, in a letter to Senator Pomeroy, bluntly rejected colonization: "The children of the black man have enriched the soil by their tears, and sweat, and blood. Sir, we were born here, and we choose to remain."[38] Salmon P. Chase, Lincoln's secretary of the treasury, wrote in his diary, "How much better would be a manly protest against prejudice against color!—and a wise effort to give freemen homes in America!"[39]

A month after the meeting with the black delegation, Lincoln issued the Preliminary Emancipation Proclamation, stating that "the effort to colonize persons of African descent, with their consent, upon this continent, or elsewhere, with the previously obtained consent of the Governments existing there, will be continued."[40] The announcement of emancipation overshadowed the detail about colonization, which drew relatively little attention in the press.[41] One Republican paper, the *Cincinnati Commercial*, argued the proclamation was not radical, noting that Lincoln declared "in favor of the policy of colonization, having no disposition to allow the emancipated negroes to be thrust upon unwilling communities."[42]

At two meetings of free African Americans in New York City, the response to the proclamation's promise of colonization was hostile. At a meeting at the Bridge Street Methodist Church in Brooklyn, J. W. B. Smith was pained to hear from Lincoln that "his race and theirs could never dwell together in this land in terms of equality." Smith panned the proposed Chiriquí colonization scheme: "Why send us to Chiriqui—a place which, if Satan himself had been sent to search, he could not have selected a worse" one. The Reverend James N. Gloucester criticized all colonization schemes for "expatriating the colored people from the land of their birth, as unnecessary, impolitic and unjust." The Reverend Thompson pointed out that black people would never leave the country in large numbers. Some might leave to escape racist violence or to better their condition, but "the idea that the mass of the colored population would willingly leave their homes and their native land was preposterous, and might as well be dismissed, once for all."[43] At a reception for Robert Smalls, the black boat pilot who had commandeered a Confederate vessel and escaped to freedom with his crew and their families, speakers commended Smalls for his heroic act. Their "gallant brother" upended the assumptions underlying colonization. Smalls represented a "faithful devotedness to the cause of the American Union," and his act illustrated "the conduct of the black citizens of the United States."[44]

Lincoln's last public pronouncement on colonization came in his annual message to Congress on December 1, 1862, by which time the Central American republics had rejected all colonization schemes.[45] A treaty that would have paved the way for colonization in Mexico failed in the Senate in July 1862.[46] Lincoln hinted at the problems arising from the Chiriquí colonization project as "several of the Spanish-American republics" had protested emigrants being sent to their territories. Lincoln said he would not establish a colony in any country without obtaining consent of that country and its agreement to "receive and protect such emigrants in all the rights of freemen." Liberia and Haiti "as yet" were the only countries where black emigrants "could go with certainty of being received and adopted as citizens."

Lincoln conceded there was not much enthusiasm from free African Americans to leave the United States, but he optimistically—and wrongly—predicted "there will be an augmented, and considerable migration," to those countries.[47]

Lincoln also proposed a constitutional amendment on gradual emancipation that included compensation if slavery were abolished by 1900 and aid for colonization. Slaves freed by "the chances of war" would be "forever free," but their owners, if not disloyal, would receive compensation; and Congress may appropriate money for resettling free black people, "with their own consent," outside the United States. The third article of the proposed amendment concerned "the future of the freed people" and authorized Congress to aid in colonization. Colonization itself would require the "mutual consent" of the people deported and the American voters.[48]

Lincoln said he could not "make it better known than it already is, that I strongly favor colonization"; however, he also hinted that he had either given up on the idea of large-scale colonization or now thought that colonization would be very gradual. Lincoln addressed "an objection urged against free colored persons remaining in the country, which is largely imaginary, if not sometimes malicious." The continued presence of free blacks, he said, would not injure or displace white labor. "If they stay in their old places, they jostle no white laborers; if they leave their old places, they leave them open to white laborers." Lincoln tried to convince white northerners that emancipation in the South would not "send the free people north." Former slaves had fled north in the past to escape bondage. If gradual emancipation and deportation were adopted, then they would have no reason to migrate north. Lincoln predicted that the newly freed slaves would work for wages until "new homes can be found for them, in congenial climes, and with people of their own blood and race." And if Lincoln was wrong and blacks moved north, then the north could "decide for itself, whether to receive them." Lincoln did not mention that Illinois with its exclusion law already had decided not to receive free blacks.[49]

The *Weekly Anglo-African* rejected Lincoln's stance on colonization: "As free colored men, we thank Mr. Lincoln for nothing, when he asks Congress to provide for the expatriation of such of us as may desire to leave the country. We are decidedly of the opinion that we will stay."[50] Horace Greeley's *New-York Daily Tribune* suggested an alternative scheme: "instead of colonizing the slaves, we should colonize the slaveholders." Slaves were "peaceable, industrious, and orderly people, whose labor we can hardly dispense with," while slaveholders were "a disorderly, idle, lazy, and troublesome set, who have kept the country in hot water for the last twenty years, and have at last, by the foulest treason and rebellion, involved it in a desperate and costly civil war."[51]

Two months after Lincoln issued his Preliminary Emancipation Proclamation, Edward Bates, his attorney general, released an opinion that addressed whether a man is "legally incapacitated to be a citizen of the United States by the sole fact that he is a colored, and not a white man." Salmon Chase had requested the opinion after a schooner was detained because a "colored man" was its master and federal law required that masters of vessels in the coastal trade be US citizens. Bates concluded that a "*free man of color* . . . if born in the United States, is a citizen of the United States." To reach this conclusion, Bates read *Dred Scott* as narrowly as possible, rejecting most of Taney's opinion as nonbinding dicta.[52] Bates's dismissal of *Dred Scott* buoyed the hopes of advocates of black citizenship such as Frederick Douglass.[53] Chase later used the opinion as authority for black suffrage.[54]

Bates noted, after eighty years of "practical enjoyment of citizenship" under the Constitution, that neither the exact meaning of the word nor its constituent elements were known. Bates did not solve this problem. According to him, a citizen under the Constitution was "a member of the body politic" who is born to "the duty of allegiance and the right of protection." Every person in the United States was born a citizen, including women and children. Bates expressed a narrow view of the attributes of citizenship, ridiculing the notion that the right to vote was "one of the constituent elements of American citizenship."[55] Like Lincoln, Bates believed the legal capacity of citizens to vote or hold office depended on the states. The *New York Times* claimed that Bates's opinion had little practical effect: it enabled free blacks to command vessels, to sue in federal court, and to obtain passports—"that is pretty much all."[56] A fervent proponent of forced colonization, Bates was embarrassed by the more liberal interpretations of his opinion.[57] After the Emancipation Proclamation, Bates's opinion on citizenship was largely overlooked.

The Declining Support for Colonization

Lincoln did not publicly campaign for colonization after he issued the Emancipation Proclamation. The planning for the colonization project at Île à Vache off the coast of Haiti began in the fall of 1862, the emigrants departed for Haiti in April 1863, and the project ended disastrously in the spring of 1864, with Lincoln sending a vessel to rescue the surviving emigrants.[58] After the twin failures of Chiriquí and Île à Vache, Lincoln turned to European countries. Potential projects in British Honduras and Dutch Suriname were part of a "second wave" of attempts launched in 1863 that "all stalled by early 1864."[59] None of these diplomatic contacts led to any emigration.[60]

In March 1864 the failure of the Île à Vache project was widely reported in northern newspapers under such headlines as "The Negro Colonies a Failure" and "Colonization Collapses."[61] The *National Anti-Slavery Standard* noted that the "head of our slow-going but honest President was for a time filled with colonization cobwebs, but the miscarriage of all his schemes, and the numerous demonstrations of the safety and practicability of emancipation have served, we hope, to clear his brains of such folly."[62] The *Liberator* in April noted that the failed experiment in Haiti was "the beginning and the end of the effort to rid ourselves of the colored population in our land." As "slow as Mr. Lincoln is in comprehending the logic of events," he must have learned the lesson of the failure of his "cherished undertaking."[63] In July, Congress repealed any appropriations for colonization except for funds necessary to fulfill existing obligations.[64] In July 1864, John Hay wrote in his diary, "I am glad the President has sloughed off that idea of colonization."[65]

Some historians believe Lincoln was feigning support for colonization to win approval for emancipation.[66] Although Lincoln is often portrayed as a masterful strategist, it is difficult to see the political brilliance in selling northern whites on emancipation because it would be packaged with colonization and then later abandoning colonization. Why would Lincoln have assumed northern whites would forget he had promised colonization? Lincoln appears to have abandoned any hope of large-scale colonization, but this was not part of a deceptive plan.

Since Lincoln had supported colonization for years, it is unclear why his public support in the first two years of his administration would have been a mere feint. He convinced his own cabinet that he supported colonization. Gideon Welles, secretary of the Navy, recalled Lincoln had "a plan for the deportation of the colored race" and "a belief, amounting to a conviction, that the two races could not dwell together in unity and as equals in their social relation." In cabinet meetings in the fall of 1862, Montgomery Blair, postmaster general, argued that it was "necessary to rid the country of its black population." Edward Bates, attorney general, argued that emancipation must be accompanied by deportation because assimilation meant amalgamation, which, in turn, meant "degradation and demoralization to the white race. The whites might be brought down, but the negroes could not be lifted to a much higher plane than they now occupied." Welles later claimed that "these were also the President's views."[67] Lincoln, however, disagreed with Bates that colonization could be coerced. Welles noted in his diary, "The President objected unequivocally to compulsion. Their emigration must be voluntary and without expense to themselves."[68]

Lincoln's insistence on a "voluntary system" was the weak link in his colonization schemes. In the 1850s Lincoln had consistently argued that blacks were entitled to their natural rights but not necessarily to any political rights. One of the most basic natural rights was mobility, which included the right to stay put. Whatever black support for emigration existed in 1861 and 1862 collapsed after the failures of Chiriquí and Île à Vache, the issuance of the Emancipation Proclamation, and the enlistment of black troops, which blacks hoped would lead to citizenship. Lincoln, in his address to black leaders in August 1862 and in his annual message to Congress later that year, conceded that few blacks were willing to emigrate.

The only evidence that Lincoln gave any serious thought to colonization after Hay's diary entry of July 1, 1864, comes from Benjamin Butler's decades-later accounts of an April 1865 meeting with Lincoln.[69] These self-serving reminiscences do not provide much support since their purpose was to rehabilitate Butler's reputation.[70] The point of most reminiscences by Lincoln's contemporaries was that the author instantly recognized Lincoln's genius; the point of Butler's reminiscences was that Lincoln instantly recognized Butler's genius.

Butler's account first appeared in a collection of reminiscences published in 1886. In this account, Lincoln sent for Butler, which seems doubtful by itself, and told Butler that he was "troubled about the negroes," who, Lincoln feared, would form guerilla parties in the South. He asked Butler, as though he was thinking about colonization for the very first time, Would it be possible "to export them to some place, say Liberia, or South America," so they might "organize themselves into communities to support themselves?" Lincoln then commanded Butler to "examine the practicability of such exportation" and report back. After a few days of examination "with the aid of statistics and calculations," Butler concluded that colonization was impracticable because the number of expatriated blacks would never be more than the natural increase of the black population in the United States. Butler shared his conclusions with Lincoln, who pored over his calculations and then "looked up sadly and said: 'Your deductions seem to be correct, General. But what can we do?'"[71] These recollected, or reimagined, conversations are preposterous. Lincoln had supported voluntary colonization; now, in Butler's account, he was for deporting *all* blacks in the United States, which he had never before supported. Lincoln was days away from calling for black suffrage; this colonization scheme was the antithesis of black citizenship.[72] The credibility of Butler's account only decreases as he goes on.

Six years later, Butler published another account of this April meeting in his memoir *Butler's Book*, which is plagued with falsehoods.[73] This account of Butler's alleged meeting with Lincoln follows the earlier one, except, remarkably, Butler's memory of what was said had only improved with the passage of time. This account is even less credible than the earlier one, because in *Butler's Book* Lincoln now makes it very clear he wants to deport all blacks.[74]

It seems likely Lincoln changed his mind about colonization sometime after he issued the Emancipation Proclamation.[75] As Lincoln's mind slowly changed on citizenship, it slowly changed on colonization. One week after the Emancipation Proclamation was issued, H. Ford Douglas predicted, "This war will educate Mr. Lincoln out of his idea of the deportation of the Negro."[76]

Military Service and Citizenship

The use of black troops led the way for black citizenship.[77] Before the war came, Lincoln had consistently separated natural rights from civil, or citizenship, rights.[78] Military service had been associated with citizenship since the American Revolution.[79] Long before the Civil War, black abolitionists advocating equal rights had highlighted black military service during the American Revolution and the War of 1812.[80] In 1836 Lincoln called for voting rights for those who served in the militia. But serving in the antebellum militia had been a white privilege. The federal militia law had been limited to free white males.[81] Similarly, Illinois limited its militia to white males.[82] The opportunity for black men to serve in the military would mean that the concept of citizen-soldier would no longer be racialized. Lincoln's attorney general, Edward Bates, a supporter of compulsory emigration, opposed black enlistment precisely because it would lead to a "better fate than to be transported to a strange land."[83]

Lincoln, like most white northerners, had thought black men lacked the requisite manly virtues to be effective soldiers. In the spring and summer of 1862, members of his cabinet, such as Secretary of War Simon Cameron and Secretary of the Treasury Salmon Chase, advocated the use of black troops, which Lincoln consistently rejected.[84] The Preliminary Emancipation Proclamation did not mention the use of black troops. The final Emancipation Proclamation did, stating that "such persons of suitable condition, will be received into the armed service of the United States to garrison forts, positions, stations, and other places, and to man vessels of all sorts in said service."[85] Lincoln did not explain why he changed his mind between September 1862 and January 1863.

Congress had paved the way for the use of black troops in July 1862 when it passed the Second Confiscation Act, which gave the president authority to employ "as many persons of African descent as he may deem necessary and proper for the suppression of this rebellion, and for this purpose he may organize and use them in such manner as he may judge best for the public welfare."[86] Lincoln initially opposed the use of black troops. Publicly, he offered political reasons.[87] When a "deputation of Western gentlemen" offered two regiments of black soldiers from Indiana in August 1862, Lincoln demurred. He stated that he could not lose the border states, and "to arm the negroes would turn 50,000 bayonets from the loyal Border States against us that were for us." He "would employ all colored men offered as laborers, but would not promise to make soldiers of them."[88] In July 1862 Lincoln told Orville H. Browning, "At present none are to be armed. It would produce dangerous & fatal dissatisfaction in our army, and do more injury than good."[89] When Frederick Douglass later pressed Lincoln on his tardiness in using black soldiers, Lincoln responded that "the measure could not have been successfully adopted at the beginning of the war; that the wisdom of making colored men soldiers was still doubted; that their enlistment was a serious offense to popular prejudice."[90]

In addition to political considerations, Lincoln had opposed arming African Americans because he believed they would quickly surrender or retreat: "But I am not so sure we could do much with the blacks. If we were to arm them, I fear that in a few weeks the arms would be in the hands of the rebels; and indeed thus far we have not had arms enough to equip our white troops."[91] Lincoln was not the only white man who held this view about black cowardice.[92] One of the reasons that white northerners like Lincoln could not accept black citizenship was that citizenship had become inextricably interwoven with notions of masculinity. White northerners believed that black men lacked manly virtues such as bravery. Edwin M. Stanton, secretary of war, noted in December 1863 that many persons had "confidently asserted that freed slaves would not make good soldiers, that they would lack courage and could not be subjected to military discipline."[93] Frederick Douglass later recast this racist argument against the use of black troops: "Besides, if you make the negro a soldier, you cannot depend on his courage; a crack of his old master's whip would send him scampering in terror from the field."[94] Less than two years after Lincoln had dismissed the very notion of black troops because of racist stereotypes, he was referring to his "black warriors."[95]

The war gave black men an opportunity to earn citizenship through military service.[96] At ceremonies honoring black troops before they went off to war, local authorities would often present an American flag to the black regiments and give speeches about how becoming a soldier had uplifted the men who donned the uniform of the Union. For example, when Governor John A. Andrew presented the colors to the Fifty-Fourth Massachusetts Infantry Regiment, he said, "Today, we recognize the right of every man in this Commonwealth to be a MAN and a citizen."[97] The regimental flag of the 127th United States Colored Troops carried the inscription "We Will Prove Ourselves Men." The regimental flag of the Twenty-Fourth United States Colored Troops carried the inscription "Let Soldiers in War, Be Citizens in Peace." To prove themselves men would prove themselves worthy of being citizens.

Later W. E. B. Du Bois observed that "proof of manhood" was "the ability and willingness to take human life." When the black man "rose and fought and killed, the whole nation with one voice proclaimed him a man and brother." Du Bois concluded that nothing else made black citizenship conceivable but the record of the black soldier as a fighter.[98] Military service provided an opportunity for black men to demonstrate their masculinity, which, in turn, provided a powerful argument for citizenship.[99]

Citizenship consisted of rights and duties. By fulfilling the duty of military service, black men would claim the rights of citizenship. Congress had already recognized that noncitizen immigrants could become citizens after military service. In July 1862, Congress included a provision that allowed any adult alien who was honorably discharged from military service to become a citizen without any previous declaration of intent, with only one year's residence instead of the five years that was usually required, and the honorable discharge itself would be proof of good moral character.[100]

Douglass clearly understood the opportunity that military service could provide: "The opportunity is given us to be men." In a July 1863 speech to raise black troops, he said, "With one courageous resolution we may blot out the hand-writing of ages against us. Once let the black man get upon his person the brass letters U.S., let him get an eagle on his button, and a musket on his shoulder, and bullets in his pocket, and there is no power on earth or under the earth which can deny that he has earned the right of citizenship in the United States."

Douglass told his audience that "nothing can be more plain, nothing more certain than that the speediest and best possible way open to us to manhood, equal rights and elevation, is that we enter this service."[101] He understood that masculinity, military service, and citizenship were all interconnected. Service in the military proved one's manhood, which, in turn, proved one's entitlement to citizenship.[102]

Women's rights activists joined the chorus for equal rights. Elizabeth Cady Stanton and Susan B. Anthony formed the Women's Loyal National League in May 1863. The organization supported Lincoln's Emancipation Proclamation, hoping it would be followed by black suffrage. The group linked black freedom with women's rights. Disappointed by Lincoln's reconstruction plan for Louisiana, Anthony and Stanton supported John C. Frémont for president. They wanted to use the anniversary meeting of the Women's Loyal National League to advance Frémont's candidacy.[103] Their call for the meeting encouraged women to make themselves "a power for freedom in the coming Presidential campaign." Caroline Dall, a women's rights leader and Garrisonian abolitionist, criticized Anthony and Stanton for wanting to turn the meeting into an "electioneering caucus" and for opposing Lincoln.[104] Cady, in turn, ridiculed Dall for "dooming women into modest silence." She proudly described the Women's Loyal National League as "the first and only organization of women for the declared purpose of influencing politics."[105] At the anniversary meeting, the group called for a constitutional amendment that would grant voting rights to all "citizens who are taxed, or who bear arms to support the Government."[106] Without a racial or gender qualification, this suffrage proposal would have ensured at least some voting by black veterans and taxpaying women. By tying voting to fulfilling obligations to the state, it rejected suffrage based on race and gender; it also oddly echoed Lincoln's 1836 statement on suffrage. The exchange between Dall and Stanton about women and the presidential race caught Lincoln's attention; he twice wrote Dall congratulatory notes.[107]

When Lincoln later told Douglass he had been tardy in using black troops because the wisdom of such a policy was doubted, he was including himself among the doubters. Lincoln's doubts may have been lessened by the arguments advanced by his cabinet members and others and by a book published in the fall of 1862 by George Livermore, *An Historical Research Respecting the Opinions of the Founders of the Republic on Negroes as Slaves, as Citizens, and as Soldiers.*[108] Livermore had researched this topic, as his friend Charles Sumner noted, "at a critical moment, before the Government had determined to enlist colored soldiers."[109] When the book was published, the *Liberator* wished it would find a place in every northern household because "it would do much towards extirpating that vulgar, cruel and unchristian prejudice which so universally prevails against the colored race."[110]

Because of the nexus between citizenship and military service, Livermore's research necessarily covered black citizenship in the founding period. Livermore quoted Taney's pronouncement that blacks were "so far inferior that they had no rights which the white man was bound to respect" and retorted, "This remarkable assertion is in direct violation of historic truth," a point that the *Dred Scott* dissenters and Lincoln had made five years earlier.[111] Livermore used arguments in the first half of his book that were very similar to arguments used by Lincoln in the 1850s.[112]

The second half of Livermore's book would have been new to Lincoln when he read it in December. When Charles Sumner sent a copy of Livermore's book to Lincoln, he called Lincoln's attention to the "last half" of the book "on the employment of Slaves & Africans during our Revolution." Sumner recommended the book as "learned, thorough & candid."[113] When Lincoln was preparing the final Proclamation of

Emancipation, he asked if Sumner could send his copy to him, as Lincoln had mislaid his own. After Livermore died in 1865, Sumner hailed Livermore's book as playing a conspicuous role in swaying the public mind on the use of black troops, noting also that it was "within my own knowledge that it much interested President Lincoln."[114]

Livermore addressed the important question now "presented to our National Government at this time, respecting the employment of negroes as soldiers." He began with the Boston Massacre, where the black martyr Crispus Attucks "was the first to fall." At the battle of Bunker Hill, "negro soldiers stood side by side, and fought bravely, with their white brethren." Freed slaves served faithfully, "their skill and bravery were never called into question, but, on the contrary, were frequently commended." Livermore concluded, "That large numbers of negroes were enrolled in the army, and served faithfully as soldiers during the whole period of the War of the Revolution, may be regarded as a well-established historical fact."[115]

Perhaps it was the confluence of advice, events, and Livermore's book, but one way or another, Lincoln changed his mind about the use of black troops. He became a proponent. In a March 1863 letter to Andrew Johnson, Lincoln wrote, "The colored population is the great *available* and yet *unavailed* of, force for restoring the Union. The bare sight of fifty thousand armed, and drilled black soldiers on the banks of the Mississippi, would end the rebellion at once."[116] In a letter to Grant in August 1863, Lincoln said, "I believe it is a resource which, if vigorously applied now, will soon close the contest. It works doubly, weakening the enemy and strengthening us."[117]

A popular racist song may have helped the cause of black soldiers, though it did so in a roundabout way. Charles G. Halpine, an officer in the Union army and a friend of Lincoln's secretary John Hay, wrote songs and stories under the pseudonym Private Miles O'Reilly.[118] As O'Reilly, Halpine published a song titled "Sambo's Right to Be Kilt" in January 1864 in the *New York Herald*. The song was addressed to whites who opposed the use of black troops. Halpine later admitted it was "extremely devoid of any philanthropic or humanitarian cant."[119] The newspaper introduced the song by noting that O'Reilly "was in the habit of saying that he has seen such a plenty of white men killed in this war that he has no objection now to letting the 'Sambos' take their fair share of death and wounds." The song proclaimed black soldiers could shoot guns and die in battle instead of whites. The first verse concluded: "I'll let Sambo be shot instead of myself / On ev'ry day in the year."[120] Within weeks, the song had been published in countless Northern newspapers.[121] Lincoln was an admirer. Hay told Halpine that, after hearing the song, Lincoln said:

> That song reminds me of what Deacon Stoddard, away down in Menard County, said one day, when a woman that was of suspected repute dropped a half eagle into the collection plate, after one of his charity sermons: "I don't know where she gets it, nor how she earns it; but the money's good, and will do good. I wish she had some better way of getting it than she is thought to have; and that those who do get their money better, could be persuaded to make half as good a use of it." I have no doubt, Hay, that O'Reilly, in whom you seem to take an interest, might be a great deal better man than he is. But that song of his is both good and will do good.[122]

Whereas Miles O'Reilly only wanted black men to "take their fair share of death and wounds," black troops soon proved their bravery under fire. In the fall of 1862, Secretary of War Stanton, without fanfare, authorized General Rufus Saxton to recruit black soldiers in South Carolina.[123] Saxton soon reported on a coastal expedition by the First South Carolina Volunteers that was a "perfect success" as the black troops fought with "coolness and bravery." Saxton said that "they seemed like men who were fighting to vindicate their manhood."[124] Stanton's year-end report in December 1863 also referred to the masculinity of the black soldiers: "The slave has proved his manhood and his capacity as an infantry soldier at Milliken's Bend, at the assault upon Port Hudson and the storming of Fort Wagner."[125]

Lincoln answered a critic of both emancipation and the use of black troops in an August 1863 public letter, a year after his patronizing lecture on colonization. Lincoln noted that some of his generals believed "purely as military opinions" that "the emancipation policy, and the use of colored troops, constitute the heaviest blow yet dealt to the rebellion; and that, at least one of those important successes, could not have been achieved when it was, but for the aid of black soldiers." Lincoln was paraphrasing a letter from Ulysses S. Grant that he had received three days earlier. Grant had written, "I have given the subject of arming the negro my hearty support. This, with the emancipation of the negro, is the heavyest blow yet given the Confederacy."[126]

Lincoln further argued that "negroes, like other people, act upon motives." If black men were to "stake their lives for us, they must be prompted by the strongest motive—even the promise of freedom. And the promise being made, must be kept." Peace would come, and blacks who had fought gallantly and whites who had opposed their service would look back differently on the Civil War. "And then, there will be some black men who can remember that, with silent tongue, and clenched teeth, and steady eye, and well-poised bayonet, they have helped mankind on to this great consummation; while, I fear, there will be some white ones, unable to forget that, with malignant heart, and deceitful speech, they have strove to hinder it," Lincoln wrote.[127] Lincoln now saw black men as soldiers, and he saw that they deserved respect.[128]

Loyalty and Allegiance

Northerners often contrasted the loyalty of black southerners with the disloyalty of white southerners. As the Civil War raged on, some northerners called for Confederates to be stripped of their rights of citizenship. Illinois Republican politician Orville H. Browning attended a rally in September 1864 where speakers called for Confederates to be forever stripped of the rights of citizenship. General Benjamin M. Prentiss swore "he would never consent that any man who had borne arms against this government should ever enjoy the rights of citizenship—that he did not recognize the Southern people as his erring brethren; and would never agree to live under the same government with them." Jack Grimshaw, who Browning noted was "drunk, and as coarse and vulgar as drunk," fumed that "not one of them should ever enjoy the rights of citizenship again—their Country should be given to the negroes, and if they didn't like to live among negroes they could leave."[129]

Lincoln was no Jack Grimshaw. Under Lincoln's Ten Percent plan for wartime reconstruction, announced on December 8, 1863, he would grant a pardon and amnesty to those who had "participated in the existing rebellion" (with some exceptions) provided they took an oath to "henceforth faithfully support" the Constitution and all congressional laws and presidential proclamations that referred to slaves. After 10 percent of the number of voters cast in the 1860 presidential election took the oath, then "qualified voters," as defined by the election laws of the state immediately before secession, could "re-establish" the state's government. Lincoln excluded only civil and diplomatic officers and military and naval officers of the "so-called Confederate government" from holding office.[130]

Lincoln's was not the only plan in the works. The reconstruction plan introduced in Congress in February 1864 by Senator Benjamin F. Wade of Ohio and Representative Henry Winkler Davis of Maryland took a more restrictive approach to who could be part of the reorganized state governments. They called for federal marshals to enroll "all white male citizens" to take an oath to support the Constitution. Once a majority of those enrolled took the oath, these "loyal" citizens would elect delegates to a convention to reestablish the state government. Anyone who had held any civil or military office "under the rebel usurpation" or had "voluntarily borne arms against the United States" would be unable to take the "ironclad" oath. The convention would be required to adopt a provision that barred high-ranking military officers or government officials from voting or being governor or a member of the legislature. Finally, anyone who continued to hold certain state or confederate positions was declared "not to be a citizen of the United States." Lincoln pocket-vetoed the Wade-Davis bill in July 1864.[131]

Prior to these competing reconstruction plans, the Enrollment Act, passed by Congress in March 1863, defined two groups liable for "military duty" when "called out" by the president: "all able-bodied male citizens of the United States, and persons of foreign birth who shall have declared on oath their intention to become citizens." Under US naturalization law, aliens had to be residents for five years before they were eligible for citizenship; however, three years before admission as citizens, they had to declare their intent to become a citizen before a federal or state court.[132] While it applied to declarant aliens, the 1863 act did not apply to newly arrived or non-declarant immigrants.

Not two months later, Lincoln addressed the problem of immigrants shirking their responsibilities under the act. Lincoln was on to something: The number of immigrants serving as soldiers was far less, proportionally, than that of other groups who served.[133] Lincoln noted that some immigrants who had declared their intent to become citizens but had not yet "exercised the right of suffrage or any other political franchise" were renouncing their intent to become citizens. Lincoln ordered that "no plea of alienage" be allowed as an exemption from the military draft for any "person of foreign birth" who had declared intent to become a citizen and who remained in the United States sixty-five days from the date of his proclamation or anyone who had declared his intent to become a citizen and had "exercised, at any time, the right of suffrage, or any other political franchise."[134]

In his 1863 annual message to Congress, Lincoln complained again of immigrants who had either "declared their intention to become citizens, or who have been fully naturalized" but had evaded their military duties by denying their status. When this occurred, the government was often unable to meet its burden of proof. Because many immigrants who disavowed their ties to the United States had exercised "the right of suffrage," Lincoln suggested making "the fact of voting an estoppel against any plea of exemption from military service, or other civil obligation, on the ground of alienage."[135] Draft eligibility for declarant aliens made sense to Lincoln and congressional lawmakers because those immigrants had received a "precitizenship status": they were what historian Hiroshi Motomura has called "Americans in waiting."[136]

Immigrants in the western territories who declared their intention to become citizens found themselves eligible to become landowners. The May 1862 Homestead Act granted 160 acres of public lands to settlers to cultivate for five years and then receive title. The act fulfilled a promise in the 1860 Republican platform and benefited both citizens and declarant immigrants.[137] Voting rights in the newly organized territories were given not only to citizens but to "every white male inhabitant" in the Idaho Territory (1863) and "those who have declared their intentions" to become citizens in the Montana Territory (1864).[138]

During the war, immigrants were welcomed in the North because they were needed as laborers as well as soldiers. The 1864 platform of the National Union (Republican) Party stated that immigration "should be fostered and encouraged by a liberal and just policy." Lincoln declared in his 1864 message to Congress that immigrants were "one of the principal replenishing streams which are appointed by Providence to repair the ravages of internal war, and its wastes of national strength and health." Lincoln also made it clear that newly arriving immigrants would not be drafted, as the government "neither needs nor designs to impose involuntary military service upon those who come from other lands to cast their lot in our country."[139] Congress had encouraged enlistment by newly arrived immigrants by permitting aliens who were honorably discharged from military service to petition for citizenship without any previous declaration of intent and with only one year's residence.[140] Lincoln was assuring potential immigrants—whose labor was needed by the North—that military service was their choice.

Military service was, however, an obligation of citizens and citizens-in-waiting. If drafted, one was required to answer the call—yet more than one-fifth of those drafted failed to report.[141] In March 1865, Congress amended the Enrollment Act to punish those who failed to report and those who deserted from military or naval service. Under the law, draft dodgers and deserters would be given sixty days from the date of a presidential proclamation to either report or return. If they failed to do so, then they would be deemed to have voluntarily relinquished their rights of citizenship or their right to become a citizen and would be "forever incapable of holding any office of trust or profit under the United States, or of exercising any right of citizens thereof."[142] One week later, Lincoln dutifully issued a Proclamation Offering Pardon to Deserters.[143] Efforts to prevent deserters from voting would later be unsuccessful because courts required the proof of a court-martial.[144]

Black Men in the White House

To counter a rumor that he had once told a group of free blacks in Cincinnati he rejected all legal distinctions based on color and endorsed black suffrage, Lincoln observed, "I was never in a meeting of negroes in my life."[145] That would change once he became president. Lincoln's views on black citizenship also changed, and that is not coincidental.[146] Before he became president, Lincoln had a limited understanding of black life, though he was in frequent contact with black women and men. He employed African American women as domestic servants, and at least twenty-one black people lived within a three-block radius of the Lincoln home.[147]

Springfield barber William Fleurville, Billy the Barber, is often nominated for the role of Lincoln's "black friend."[148] Black barbers had a unique place in antebellum America; they were friendly with their white customers, despite their subordinate status, and were able to speak directly with some of the most powerful men of the time.[149] Fleurville seems to have played this role with Lincoln. While Lincoln had represented Fleurville in legal matters, his letters about Fleurville reflect a certain bemusement about his barber.[150] In the White House, Lincoln told a story about "a black barber in Illinois, notorious for lying," which seems to describe Fleurville.[151]

In any event, most of the black population in Illinois worked in menial or domestic occupations, so it was not until Lincoln reached Washington that he encountered blacks who were not servants or engaged in low-status work.[152] In Washington, Lincoln met, for the first time, African Americans who had "political experience and wide-ranging accomplishments." These encounters helped Lincoln change his outlook about the place of blacks in American society.[153] After Lincoln met with Martin R. Delany, who encouraged him to appoint black officers as a means of enlisting more southern blacks, he wrote Stanton, "Do not fail to have an interview with this most extraordinary and intelligent black man."[154]

The most famous black visitor to the Lincoln White House was Frederick Douglass.[155] Lincoln and Douglass met twice at the White House. Douglass described his meetings with Lincoln several times in speeches during the Civil War and later in reminiscences published in the 1880s. In speeches at the Cooper Institute in 1863 and at an American Anti-Slavery Society meeting in 1864, Douglass described in some detail his first meeting with the president in August 1863. He told both audiences that they might want to know how the president of the United States received a black man at the White House: "I will tell you how he received me—just as you have seen one gentleman receive another; with a hand and a voice well-balanced between a kind cordiality and a respectful reserve. I tell you I felt big there!"[156]

When Douglass introduced himself, Lincoln reached out his hand and said, "Mr. Douglass, I know you; I have read about you, and Mr. Seward has told me about you." Lincoln also admitted to Douglass that he had read one of Douglass's articles claiming that the "most sad and most disheartening feature in our present political and military situation" was "the tardy, hesitating, vacillating policy of the President of the United States." Lincoln said that this criticism was not apt because once he had taken a position, he did not retreat from it. Douglass mentioned to his audiences that when Lincoln responded to his criticism, he began with "Mr. Douglass." Douglass stated, "Think of the President of the United States addressing a black man as Mr. Douglass."[157]

Douglass recounted in some detail the matters he and Lincoln had discussed. Douglass said Lincoln had been "somewhat slow in proclaiming equal protection to our colored soldiers and sailors." Lincoln countered that the country was not ready, and it "needed talking up to that point." Lincoln also told Douglass that "the colored man throughout this country was a despised man, a hated man." If Lincoln had issued a proclamation too early, then "all the hatred which is poured on the head of the negro race would be visited on this administration." Preparatory work had been needed, and it had been done. Lincoln reminded Douglass that the battles of Milliken's Bend, Port Hudson, and Fort Wagner—where black troops had fought valiantly—were recent events.[158]

In his 1882 memoir, Douglass provided even more detail about what was discussed between the "ex-slave, identified with a despised race" and the "most exalted person in the great republic." Douglass had been helping raise black troops, and he wanted to explain to Lincoln why that was not an easy task. Douglass's early success as a military recruiter had fallen off. Potential recruits believed the government would not deal fairly with them. When Lincoln asked for details, Douglass raised three matters: unequal pay, the Confederate treatment of black prisoners, and the unavailability of recognition and promotion for "great and uncommon service on the battle-field."[159] Douglass quoted from the "all the world's a stage" monologue from *As You Like It*—black soldiers were seeking "the bubble reputation / Even in the cannon's mouth."[160] Quoting Shakespeare to Lincoln could only have helped Douglass's case.[161] Unlike the meeting on colonization a year earlier with the "deputation of Negroes," in which Lincoln had given a lecture, here Lincoln listened "with patience and silence."[162]

Lincoln, perhaps for the first time in his life, took a black man's argument on politics seriously, and he gave Douglass the respect of a thoughtful (albeit, for Douglass, unconvincing) response. He countered that "the employment of colored troops at all was a great gain to the colored people."[163] Lincoln tried to deflect the unequal pay issue by pointing out that "it was not believed that a negro could make a good soldier, as good a soldier as a white man, and hence it was thought that he should not have the same pay as a white man." Lincoln assured Douglass that "in the end they shall have the same pay as white soldiers."[164]

Retaliation was a more difficult matter, asserted Lincoln. He was afraid that Union retaliation for Confederates executing captured black troops would make matters worse, and he had heard that black troops were now being treated as prisoners of war. On the promotion of black soldiers, Lincoln had less difficulty. He told Douglass he would sign any commissions that his secretary of war commended to him. Douglass was not entirely satisfied with Lincoln's answers, but Lincoln had impressed him. Douglass also counted on the "educating tendency of the conflict" to guide Lincoln further in the future.[165] After meeting with Lincoln and Stanton, Douglass concluded that he would continue to recruit black troops because "the true course to the black man's freedom and citizenship was over the battle-field."[166]

A year later, Lincoln met with Douglass a second time. He wanted Douglass's advice on the best way to encourage "slaves in the Rebel States to come within the federal lines." Lincoln was not optimistic about his chances for reelection at this time; he told Douglass he was afraid a premature peace would come that would leave in slavery all those who had not yet come within Union lines. He said, "the slaves are not coming so rapidly and so numerously to us as I had hoped." Douglass said slaveholders knew how to keep such things from their slaves. At Lincoln's suggestion, Douglass agreed to organize "a band of scouts, composed of colored men" who would go into "the Rebel states, beyond the lines of our armies, and carry the news of emancipation, and urge the slaves to come into our boundaries."[167] After meeting with Lincoln, Douglass conferred with some "trustworthy and Patriotic Colored men," who all agreed it was a good idea. Since "every slave who escapes from the Rebel states is a loss to the Rebellion and a gain to the Loyal Cause," Douglass sent Lincoln an outline that detailed how such an effort could be implemented.[168]

Douglass saw Lincoln for the last time on the day of his second inauguration. Although black people had been barred from all previous receptions at the White House, Douglass decided he would go that evening: "it seemed now that freedom had become the law of the republic, now that colored men were on the battle-field mingling their blood with that of white men in one common effort to save the country, it was not too great an assumption for a colored man to offer his congratulations to the President with those of other citizens." When Douglass reached the door, he was stopped by two police officers, who told him that their orders were "to admit no person of my color." Douglass told the officers that no such order could have come from President Lincoln and that the president would want him to attend. When a white man was admitted who recognized Douglass, Douglass asked him to tell "Mr. Lincoln that Frederick Douglass is detained by officers at the door." Less than a minute later, Douglass was invited into the East Room of the White House. When Lincoln saw him approach, he said loudly, "Here comes my friend Douglass." After shaking Douglass's hand, Lincoln asked him about his inaugural address because "there is no man in the country whose opinion I value more than yours." Douglass responded, "Mr. Lincoln, it was a sacred effort." Lincoln replied, "I am glad you liked it!"[169]

Douglass later observed that Lincoln was free "from popular prejudice against the colored race." Lincoln was the first great man he had talked to in the United States "who in no single instance reminded me of the difference between himself and myself, of the difference of color, and I thought that all the more remarkable because he came from a state where there were black laws." Douglass believed that Lincoln's kindness toward him was "because of the similarity with which I had fought my way up, we both starting at the lowest round of the ladder."[170] Lincoln and Douglass saw each other as self-made men.

Lincoln also entertained a delegation of black men from Louisiana, where the issue of black citizenship was raised. New Orleans had a large free-black community whose members were primarily educated property owners. Arnold Bertonneau, who would later meet with Lincoln, described New Orleans as a city with "upwards of 20,000 free persons of color," nearly all of them able to read and write and many of them "being highly educated and quite wealthy."[171] These New Orleans residents demanded the right to vote as part of what Lincoln called the "free-state reorganization of Louisiana."[172]

The free blacks of New Orleans prepared a petition with more than a thousand signatures to present to both Lincoln and Congress. Arnold Bertonneau and Jean Baptiste Roudanez were selected as the members of the delegation who would take the petition to Washington. Roudanez later said their "mission with the President was to obtain the elective franchise."[173] The petition stated that most of the petitioners were owners of real property, and all of them owned personal property, and "many of them were engaged in the pursuits of commerce and industry." For nearly fifty years, they had never ceased to be "peaceable citizens, paying their taxes on an assessment of more than fifteen millions of dollars." These "loyal and devoted" men also served the Union as soldiers and would defend it "so long as their hands have strength to hold a musket." The petition requested voting rights only for those "born free before the rebellion." Bertonneau and Roudanez added a "memorial" to the petition requesting that the right of suffrage be extended "not only to natives of Louisiana of African descent born free, but also to all others, whether born slave or free, especially those who have vindicated their right to vote by bearing arms, subject only to such qualifications as shall equally affect the white and colored citizens."[174]

Bertonneau and Roudanez made a favorable impression on Lincoln during their interview with him. Bertonneau was a wine merchant, and Roudanez was a machinist and engineer.[175] The former provost marshal of New Orleans introduced Roudanez to Lincoln "as one of the most wealthy and influential citizens of Louisiana." The correspondent for an Ohio newspaper noted these two "French Creoles" had "quite dark complexions, yet European cast of features." Roudanez was educated in Paris, and both men presented "the appearance of quite scholarly patronages and polished gentlemen." According to Bertonneau, Lincoln listened attentively to his visitors and "sympathized with our object."[176]

Lincoln explained that his primary aim was to restore the Union. To achieve his goal, he would be guided by "political necessity," not "any moral aspects of the case." Because suffrage did not affect the relation of the state to the Union, granting "the free people of color" in Louisiana "the voting privilege" was of a moral nature. Lincoln said he would decline to take "any steps in the manner until a political exigency rendered such a course proper."[177] Lincoln did admit that "if he was convinced that it was necessary, in order to secure the restoration of Louisiana that they should be allowed to vote, he would do it."[178]

Lincoln wrote to Michael Hahn, the new governor of Louisiana, later that month. After congratulating Hahn for being elected "the first-free-state Governor of Louisiana," Lincoln noted that soon Louisiana would have a constitutional convention that would "probably define the elective franchise." Lincoln "barely" suggested to Hahn "whether some of the colored people may not be let in—as, for instance, the very intelligent, and especially those who have fought gallantly in our ranks." Lincoln may have seen black suffrage as a political necessity, telling Hahn that black voters "would probably help, in some trying time to come, to keep the jewel of liberty within the family of freedom."[179] Bertonneau and Roudanez's mission was not a complete success. They had called for impartial suffrage—the same qualifications for voting would apply to black and white voters. Lincoln instead called for limited suffrage—black voters might be "enfranchised by special qualifications that would not apply to whites."[180]

The Louisiana Constitution failed to provide suffrage for black men; it instead authorized the legislature to grant suffrage "as by military service, by taxation to support the government, or by intellectual fitness." The constitution did mandate public education of "all children of the state," called for "all able-bodied men" to be armed and disciplined for service in the militia, and ensured all defendants in criminal prosecutions would have the right to testify and be able to call witnesses, implicitly removing testimonial exclusions owing to race.[181]

In April 1864, a delegation of black southerners from North Carolina met with Lincoln at the White House. Led by Abraham Galloway, the group wanted to use the leverage that came from the North's growing reliance on black troops to press for black citizenship.[182] The petition presented to Lincoln recalled how free black men had voted in North Carolina until 1835 and declared that some of the northern states, "most advanced in arts, sciences, and civilization, have extended that right to the colored citizens with eminent success and good results." The petitioners asked Lincoln to finish "the noble work you have begun, and grant unto your petitioners that greatest of privileges, when the State is reconstructed, to exercise the right of suffrage."[183]

The delegation spoke very positively about their interview with Lincoln at meetings in New York City in May and back home in New Bern in June. J. R. Good told the crowd at New Bern that Lincoln had received them cordially and spoke with them "freely and kindly." He relayed Lincoln's words to the delegation: "He said that he had labored hard and through many difficulties for the good of the colored race, and that he should continue to do so, and in this matter would do what he could for us, but as a matter belonging to the State it would have to be attended to in the reconstruction of the State. He was glad to see colored men seeking for their rights, and said this was an important right which we, as a people, ought to have."[184] Clinton D. Pearson reported that Lincoln "gave the committee full assurance of his sympathy in the struggle the colored people of North Carolina are now making for their rights."[185]

For the Reverend Isaac K. Felton, the most lasting impression of the visit was the group entering the White House through the front door. When he returned to New Bern, he explained to a crowd what that meant:

> [I]n 1860, to go to the door of the lowest magistrate of Craven County, and ask for the smallest right, would have insulted him, and the offender would have been told to "go in at the gate and around to the back door, that was the place for niggers." But 1864 finds us standing at the front door of the executive mansion of the President of the U.S.! What a change! We knock and the door is opened unto us. We seek the President and find him to the joy and comfort of our hearts. We ask, and receive his sympathies and promises to do all for us all he could. He didn't tell us to go round to the back door, but, like a true gentleman and noble-hearted chief, with as much courtesy and respect as though we had been the Japanese Embassy he invited us into the White House. And after a lengthy talk with him on matters and things we again joined hands, took a hearty shake and bid farewell![186]

After meeting with Lincoln in October 1864, Sojourner Truth similarly remarked that she "never was treated by any one with more kindness and cordiality."[187]

Lincoln was open to meeting black leaders—he was "the first American president to treat African Americans as constituents." The White House was not as consistently welcoming to African Americans at public parties and receptions. The organizers of Lincoln's second inaugural ball banned black guests. But William O. Stoddard, an assistant to Lincoln, witnessed two black men attending a reception at the White House, which Stoddard described as "a practical assertion of negro citizenship, for which few were prepared." Lincoln "received them with marked kindness."[188]

Lincoln's meetings with Douglass and the delegations from New Orleans and North Carolina may have diminished his support for colonization and increased his support for black citizenship. These changes are tied together, as support for colonization would be inversely proportional to support for citizenship. Abolitionists had long recognized that colonization was the greatest obstacle to black people gaining citizenship.[189]

Black leaders in their quest for citizenship had argued for respectability, believing that white prejudice would be overcome when whites associated with blacks who exhibited white middle-class values. By meeting "upstanding" free blacks, whites would change their negative impressions and be able to accept them on equal terms.[190] Respectability politics may have worked with Lincoln. During his presidency, Lincoln's interactions with African Americans changed. He had treated the "deputation" on colonization with condescension; he treated Douglass and the New Orleans and North Carolina delegations with respect. He had lectured the first group; he conversed with Douglass, Bertonneau and Roudanez, and Galloway.

The Call for Black Citizenship

In his last public address, Lincoln said that it was "unsatisfactory to some that the elective franchise is not given to the colored man" in Louisiana. Referencing the constitutional qualifications for black suffrage, Lincoln said he would "prefer that it were now conferred on the very intelligent, and on those who serve our cause as soldiers."[191] Edward D. Neill, a secretary at the White House, believed "Mr. Lincoln preferred intelligent, impartial suffrage, without respect to color, but was willing to give the right to vote to all colored men who had been soldiers of the United States, even if they could not read."[192] Lincoln was suggesting that the Louisiana legislature use the authority conferred upon it by the state's new constitution.

Nearly thirty years before, Lincoln had been unwilling to extend suffrage to all white males; he had called for suffrage only for militia members and taxpayers. Accepting the limitations contained in the new Louisiana Constitution because states would still define citizenship, Lincoln called for black men to be enfranchised based on military service and intelligence. Lincoln did not mention tax-paying, the third possible prerequisite for black suffrage under the Louisiana Constitution. Lincoln had expressed reservations about the intelligence of freed slaves three years earlier in his address on colonization. There, he had contrasted the intelligence of free black people with slaves whose intellects were "clouded by slavery." Free black men in the District of Columbia were "capable of thinking like white men," unlike "those who have been systematically oppressed."[193] For purposes of suffrage, Lincoln divided black men in Louisiana into three categories: those who had served in the military, those who were free before the war began, and those who were newly freed. The first two groups would be able to vote, and the third group presumptively would not.

The "very intelligent" restriction probably meant requiring black men who did not serve as soldiers to take a literacy test. Such tests were not widespread either before or during the Civil War. During the nativist surges in the 1840s and 1850s, seven states had considered adding a literacy requirement for suffrage. Only two states—Connecticut and Massachusetts—had adopted such provisions.[194] On January 10, 1865, Republican representative William D. Kelley proposed an amendment to James M. Ashley's oft-amended reconstruction bill that would have allowed unrestricted suffrage to all white male citizens, but "all other male citizens" would have to be able to read the Constitution.[195] (Such devices would be used later in the Jim Crow South to disenfranchise black voters.)[196] The problem with using a literacy test with former slaves was that few slaves were literate; teaching them how to read had been prohibited.[197]

Lincoln's call for limited black suffrage was historic: this was the first time any president had publicly endorsed any form of black suffrage.[198] Lincoln had come a long way in a relatively short period of time. Under his Ten Percent plan, announced in December 1863, only whites would have been able to vote in the restored southern states.[199] But, in April 1865, for the first time since 1836, Lincoln was not in the mainstream politically on suffrage. Congress had failed to pass any legislation that favored black suffrage during the Civil War.[200] When, in March 1863, Congress organized the Idaho Territory, voting was restricted to white males.[201] One year later, after the House of Representatives voted to organize the Montana Territory and again limited suffrage to white males, the Senate removed the racial restriction. The House then insisted on limiting voting to white males. Unlike the Idaho Territory law, the Montana Territory legislation did not explicitly limit suffrage to "every free white male inhabitant." It instead incorporated the restriction from the Idaho Territory act, obscuring its intent by stating that all those "otherwise described and qualified under the fifth section" of the Idaho Territory act could vote in the Montana Territory.[202] Also that spring, an attempt to allow black suffrage in elections in the District of Columbia was defeated in the House of Representatives.[203]

Radical Republican James Ashley of Ohio introduced a reconstruction bill in December 1864 that would have extended suffrage to "every male citizen of the United States." According to Lincoln's secretary John Hay, Lincoln opposed the provisions of the bill that permitted making black men "jurors & voters under the temporary governments."[204] Ashley subsequently abandoned universal male suffrage in favor of loyal white males and black Union veterans.[205] The Wade-Davis bill, introduced in February 1864 and pocket-vetoed by Lincoln that July, also did not call for black suffrage in reconstructed states. The bill did provide that "the laws for the trial and punishment of white persons shall extend to all persons"; juries, however, would have remained all white.[206]

Consequently, Lincoln's call for limited black suffrage was momentous. At least one member of the crowd understood the significance of Lincoln's words that day. John Wilkes Booth, who was in the crowd, turned to a friend and said, "That means nigger citizenship. Now, by God, I will put him through. That will be the last speech he will ever make."[207]

CONCLUSION: "THE GREAT TASK REMAINING"

Lincoln's efforts for limited black suffrage were left unfinished. When he died, the Thirteenth Amendment was not yet ratified, so slavery would not be formally abolished in the United States until December 1865. A year after Lincoln's death, Congress passed the Civil Rights Act over Andrew Johnson's veto. The act declared that "all persons born in the United States" were "citizens of the United States."[1] The two Reconstruction amendments that addressed citizenship also came after Lincoln's death. The Fourteenth Amendment, which Congress passed in June 1866, was ratified in July 1868 and contained the promise of equal citizenship. It gave birthright citizenship a constitutional foundation and prohibited states from abridging "the privileges or immunities of citizens of the United States" or depriving "any person of life, liberty, or property, without due process of law" or denying any person "the equal protection of the laws." The Fifteenth Amendment, ratified in 1870, declared that the right of citizens to vote could not be denied "on account of race, color, or previous condition of servitude."[2] Voting rights remained gendered, however. Wendell Phillips told women's rights advocates to be patient: "But this hour belongs to the negro. As Abraham Lincoln said, 'One war at a time'; so I say, One question at a time."[3]

For most of his political career, Lincoln's answer to the question of who belonged to the political community was the mainstream northern position. But his first and last statements on citizenship were decidedly out of step with his contemporaries. In 1836 he rejected the universal white male suffrage enshrined in the 1818 Illinois Constitution and called for suffrage to be limited to taxpayers and militia members. Lincoln accepted that only whites should vote, but he would have allowed white women who paid taxes to vote, a stance that was, in its own way, anachronistic. In 1836 and 1840, Lincoln joined in race-baiting attacks on Martin Van Buren because of his support for limited black suffrage at the 1821 New York Constitutional Convention. Both Whigs and Democrats rejected the notion of black citizenship. As a Whig and later as a Republican, Lincoln rejected nativism and criticized attempts to make it more difficult for naturalized citizens to vote. Whether native-born or naturalized, all citizens would be bound together by a common belief in the principles of the Declaration of Independence. As president, Lincoln favored the "civilization" policy of assimilating Native Americans.

Lincoln continued to reject black citizenship throughout the 1850s. He hoped slavery's gradual demise would be accompanied by the gradual relocation of black people outside the United States, which placed again him in the mainstream of northern thought. These views about colonization changed during the Civil War as did his views about black citizenship. In a speech two months after Lincoln's death, Frederick Douglass said, "Lincoln soon outgrew his colonization ideas and schemes and came to look upon the Black man as an American citizen."[4] As W. E. B. Du Bois astutely observed, Lincoln "was big enough to be inconsistent."[5]

After Reconstruction ended in 1877, white supremacy was again ascendant in the South. Black disenfranchisement followed in the era of segregation. A Second Reconstruction saw a string of notable court victories and the passage of the Civil Rights Act of 1964 and the Voting Rights Act of 1965.

At Gettysburg, Lincoln saw that "the great task remaining before us" was "a new birth of freedom." More than 150 years after Lincoln's death, the struggle for full citizenship is far from over. It remains "unfinished work."[6]

ACKNOWLEDGMENTS

I want to thank Bruce Levine, John Lupton, and Michael Burlingame for reading portions of the manuscript and Charles Hubbard for originally asking me to write about Lincoln and citizenship. I thank Sylvia Frank Rodrigue and Richard W. Etulain, the editors of the Concise Lincoln Library series, for their forbearance and many helpful comments. Thanks go to Robert Brown for his careful copy editing. Kail Hidalgo provided helpful proofreading. Wayne K. Larsen, Linda Jorgensen Buhman, Jennifer Egan, and Chelsey Harris at SIU Press were all great to work with. I was fortunate to be able to develop the themes of this book at presentations at Lincoln Memorial University, St. Mary's University School of Law, and Texas Southern University Thurgood Marshall School of Law.

At South Texas College of Law Houston, Felicia Escalera and Monica Ortale of the Fred Parks Law Library tracked down obscure sources. Teri May made finishing the manuscript possible. I appreciate the camaraderie of my colleagues John Bauman, Derek Fincham, Mandi Gibson, Shelby Moore, Phillip Page, Cherie Taylor, Peter Wisniowski, and John Worley. Houston artist Sylvia Roman's *El Musico* inspired the colors used in the cover art.

I have learned a lot from volunteering at citizenship forums, and I want to acknowledge some of the great people I've worked with: Jill Campbell, Samantha Chapa, Kenia Colon, Leslie Crow, Monica Ortiz Holtkamp, Crystal Yesenia Gonzalez, Sacha Lazarre, Ana Mac Naught, Ana Osornio, Anna Gabriela Patrick, Frances Valdez, and Marisol Valero from BakerRipley; Eva Hervert, Rafael Palafox, and Claudia Ortega Hogue from the National Association of Latino Elected and Appointed Officials; and Benito Juarez from the City of Houston Office of Immigrant and Refugee Affairs.

I thank Pastor Rudy Rasmus and my church family at St. John's Downtown for their encouragement.

Most of all, I thank my spouse, Lee, and my daughters, Hannah and Emma, for their love and support.

NOTES

A Note on Online Sources

Accessing primary sources about Lincoln and his age has never been easier. Lincoln's *Collected Works*, published in 1953, is now online and searchable (quod.lib.umich.edu/l/lincoln/). The Abraham Lincoln Papers at the Library of Congress have been digitized and include incoming correspondence (www.loc.gov/collections/abraham-lincoln-papers/). The comprehensive Lincoln Legal Papers are online and searchable (www.lawpracticeofabraham lincoln.org/). The Library of Congress also has digitized the Frederick Douglass Papers (www.loc.gov/collections/frederick-douglass-papers/). Douglass's June 1865 Lincoln eulogy apparently is not available online, but Emma Steiner graciously tracked down that speech for me. The *Sangamo Journal* / *Illinois Journal* and other Illinois newspapers can be found at the Illinois Digital Newspaper Collection (idnc.library.illinois.edu/). The Library of Congress also hosts Chronicling America, which links to digitized newspapers (chroniclingamerica.loc.gov/). The complete archive for the *New York Times*, which begins in 1851, is available to subscribers (timesmachine. nytimes.com). The Western Illinois University Library has collected the laws of Illinois, including revised and compiled statutes and the laws passed by each general assembly (www.wiu.edu/libraries/govpubs/illinois_laws/index .php). Almost every nineteenth-century book cited in the notes was found online at Google Books (books.google.com/), Archive.org, or HathiTrust (www.hathitrust.org/).

Introduction: "My Fellow Citizens"

1. Abraham Lincoln [Lincoln hereinafter], "Communication to the People of Sangamo County," March 9, 1832, in *The Collected Works of Abraham Lincoln*, ed. Roy Basler, 8 vols. (New Brunswick, NJ: Rutgers University Press, 1953), 1:5; Lincoln, "Response to Serenade," April 10, 1865, *Collected Works*, 8:393; Michael Vorenberg, "Abraham Lincoln's 'Fellow Citizens'—before and after Emancipation," in *Lincoln's Proclamation: Emancipation Reconsidered*, ed. William A. Blair and Karen Fisher Younger (Chapel Hill: University of North Carolina Press, 2009), 151–69.
2. Harold Holzer, *Lincoln President-Elect: Abraham Lincoln and the Great Secession Winter 1860–1861* (New York: Simon and Schuster, 2008), 389–90.
3. Lincoln, "Speech at Pittsburgh, Pennsylvania," February 15, 1861, *Collected Works*, 4:210–13.
4. Lincoln, "Speech from the Steps of the Capitol at Columbus, Ohio," February 13, 1861, *Collected Works*, 4:205–6.

5. E.g., Lincoln, "Remarks at Hudson, New York," February 19, 1861, *Collected Works*, 4:228; Lincoln, "Remarks at Westfield, New York," February 16, 1861, *Collected Works*, 4:219.
6. Lincoln, "Remarks at Painesville, Ohio," February 16, 1861, *Collected Works*, 4:218; Lincoln, "Remarks at Newark, Ohio," February 14, 1861, *Collected Works*, 4:206.
7. Lincoln, "Speech to Germans at Cincinnati, Ohio," February 12, 1861, *Collected Works*, 4:201–2.
8. Lincoln, "Speech in Independence Hall, Philadelphia, Pennsylvania," February 22, 1861, *Collected Works*, 4:240.
9. "The President Elect on Washington's Birthday in Independence Hall," *New York Herald*, February 23, 1861, 6.
10. Douglas Bradburn, *The Citizenship Revolution: Politics and the Creation of the American Union 1774–1804* (Charlottesville: University of Virginia Press, 2009); James H. Kettner, *The Development of American Citizenship, 1608–1870* (Chapel Hill: University of North Carolina Press, 1978); William J. Novak, "The Legal Transformation of Citizenship in Nineteenth-Century America," in *The Democratic Experiment: New Directions in American Political History*, ed. Meg Jacobs, William J. Novak, and Julian E. Zelizer (Princeton, NJ: Princeton University Press, 2003), 85–119; Rogers Smith, *Civic Ideals: Conflicting Visions of Citizenship in U.S. History* (New Haven, CT: Yale University Press, 1997).
11. *Opinion of Attorney General Bates on Citizenship* (Washington, DC: Government Printing Office, 1863), 3.
12. Perez v. Brownell, 356 U.S. 44, 64 (1958) (Warren, C. J., dissenting opinion).
13. Eric Foner, *The Second Founding: How the Civil War and Reconstruction Remade the Constitution* (New York: W. W. Norton, 2019), 5–7.
14. Barbara Young Welke, *Law and the Borders of Belonging in the Long Nineteenth Century United States* (New York: Cambridge University Press, 2010), 3–9.
15. Lincoln, "To the Editor of the *Sangamo Journal*," June 18, 1836, *Collected Works*, 1:48.
16. John Bouvier, *A Law Dictionary*, 2 vols. (Philadelphia: T. and J. W. Johnson, 1839), 1:178–79; see Alexander Keyssar, *The Right to Vote: The Contested History of Democracy in the United States*, rev. ed. (New York: Basic Books, 2009), 27–28.
17. Rodney O. Davis and Douglas L. Wilson, eds., *The Lincoln-Douglas Debates* (Urbana: University of Illinois Press, 2008), 131.
18. Lincoln, "Address on Colonization to a Deputation of Negroes," August 14, 1862, *Collected Works*, 5:370–75.
19. Lincoln, "Last Public Address," April 11, 1865, *Collected Works*, 8:403.

20. On Lincoln's use of the N-word, see Henry Louis Gates Jr., ed., *Lincoln on Race and Slavery* (Princeton, NJ: Princeton University Press, 2009), xxi–xxvi.
21. Elizabeth Stordeur Pryor, "The Etymology of Nigger: Resistance, Language, and the Politics of Freedom in the Antebellum North," *Journal of the Early Republic* 36 (Summer 2016): 210.
22. David Walker, *Walker's Appeal*, 2nd ed. (Boston: printed by the author, 1830), 57.
23. H[osea] Easton, *A Treatise on the Intellectual Character, and Civil and Political Condition of the Colored People of the U. States; And the Prejudice Exercised towards Them* (Boston: Isaac Knapp, 1837), 40.
24. Pryor, "Etymology of Nigger," 227–28.

1. When Lincoln Whigged Out on Suffrage

1. *Sangamo Journal*, June 11, 1836, 2.
2. Lincoln, "To the Editor of the *Sangamo Journal*," June 18, 1836, *Collected Works*, 1:48. Other Whigs followed suit. See, e.g., "To the Editor of the *Journal*," *Sangamo Journal*, June 25, 1836, 2; "To the Voters of Sangamon County," *Sangamo Journal*, June 25, 1836, 2.
3. Illinois Constitution of 1818, art. 2, sec. 27.
4. David Donald, *Lincoln* (New York: Simon and Schuster, 1995), 59.
5. Richard Lawrence Miller cites two articles published in July 1835 and October 1836 in the *Chicago American* about "unnaturalized foreigners" voting "promiscuously." I have been unable to find any similar concerns in the *Sangamo Journal* in either year. Richard Lawrence Miller, *Lincoln and His World: Prairie Politician, 1834–1842* (Mechanicsburg, PA: Stackpole Books, 2008), 89.
6. James William Putnam, *The Illinois and Michigan Canal: A Study in Economic History* (Chicago: University of Chicago Press, 1918), 37. On the Irish canal diggers, see Ryan Dearinger, *The Filth of Progress: Immigrants, Americans, and the Building of Canals and Railroads in the West* (Oakland: University of California Press, 2015), 57–106.
7. The *Sangamo Journal* did clip a report from the *Chicago American* about 100 to 150 illegal votes in the "late election" in Chicago. *Sangamo Journal*, August 13, 1836, 2.
8. Graham Alexander Peck, "Politics and Ideology in a Free Society: Illinois from Statehood to Civil War," (PhD diss., Northwestern University, 2001), 164–65; Charles Manfred Thompson, *The Illinois Whigs before 1846* (Urbana: University of Illinois, 1915), 79; *Sangamo Journal*, September 1, 1838, 2; "Purity of Elections," *Sangamo Journal*, November 3, 1838, 2.
9. "Illinois Elections," *Sangamo Journal*, August 25, 1838, 2.
10. *Sangamo Journal*, August 18, 1838, 2.

11. "Foreign Office-Holders," *Sangamo Journal*, January 5, 1839, 3. In the following month, the Sangamon County Lyceum debated this question: "Ought Aliens be permitted to hold civil office?" *Sangamo Journal*, February 9, 1839, 3.
12. Thomas Brown, "The Miscegenation of Richard Mentor Johnson as an Issue in the National Election Campaign of 1835–1836," *Civil War History* 39 (March 1993): 5–30; William G. Shade, "'The Most Delicate and Exciting Topic': Martin Van Buren, Slavery, and the Election of 1836," *Journal of the Early Republic* 18 (Autumn 1998): 459–84.
13. "The Strength of the Case," *Sangamo Journal*, September 3, 1836, 2; *Sangamo Journal*, June 27, 1835, 1; *Sangamo Journal*, September 26, 1835, 2.
14. *Sangamo Journal*, April 9, 1836, 2; *Sangamo Journal*, June 4, 1836, 2.
15. *Sangamo Journal*, November 7, 1835, 2.
16. "The Free Negro System," *Sangamo Journal*, July 9, 1836, 2.
17. "Van Buren, Free Negro Suffrage, Property Qualifications and the Roman Catholic Religion," *Sangamo Journal*, July 30, 1836, 2.
18. *Sangamo Journal*, July 2, 1836, 2.
19. "Communications," *Sangamo Journal*, June 25, 1836, 2.
20. Michael Burlingame, *Abraham Lincoln: A Life*, 2 vols. (Baltimore: Johns Hopkins University Press, 2008), 1:109–10.
21. Douglas L. Wilson, *Lincoln before Washington: New Perspectives on the Illinois Years* (Urbana: University of Illinois Press, 1998), 56, 68.
22. William H. Herndon and Jesse W. Weik, *Herndon's Lincoln*, ed. Douglas L. Wilson and Rodney O. Davis (1892; repr., Urbana: University of Illinois Press, 2006), 143. James H. Matheny said that, as deputy postmaster, he delivered hundreds of contributions from Lincoln to the *Journal*'s offices. Douglas L. Wilson and Rodney O. Davis, eds., *Herndon's Informants: Letters, Interviews, and Statements about Abraham Lincoln* (Urbana: University of Illinois Press, 1998), 431. On Lincoln and the *Journal*, see also Glenn H. Seymour, "'Conservative': Another Lincoln Pseudonym?," *Journal of the Illinois State Historical Society* 29 (July 1936): 135–50.
23. *Sangamo Journal*, June 4, 1836, 2.
24. Pryor, "Etymology of Nigger," 227–28.
25. *Journal of the House of Representatives at the Second Session of the Ninth General Assembly* (Vandalia, IL: Sawyer, 1836), 211–13, 233.
26. *Journal of the House of Representatives*, 236–37.
27. *Journal of the House of Representatives*, 236–37.
28. *Sangamo Journal*, January 16, 1836, 2.
29. *Sangamo Journal*, April 9, 1836, 2; see also *Sangamo Journal*, July 9, 1836, 2; *Sangamo Journal*, June 25, 1836, 2.
30. Donald Ratcliffe, "The Right to Vote and the Rise of Democracy, 1787–1828," *Journal of the Early Republic* 33 (Summer 2013), 219, 245;

Chilton Williamson, *American Suffrage: From Property to Democracy, 1760–1860* (Princeton, NJ: Princeton University Press, 1960), 202; John Antony Casais, "The New York State Constitutional Convention of 1821 and Its Aftermath" (PhD diss., Columbia University, 1967).

31. Nathaniel H. Carter and William L. Stone, *Reports of the Proceedings and Debates of the Convention of 1821* (Albany, NY: E. and E. Hosford, 1821), 139, 178, 219, 284, 367, 375–76.
32. Phyllis F. Field, *The Politics of Race in New York: The Struggle for Black Suffrage in the Civil War Era* (Ithaca, NY: Cornell University Press, 1982), 37.
33. *Sangamo Journal*, July 2, 1836, 3.
34. *Sangamo Journal*, July 9, 1836, 2.
35. Davis and Wilson, *Lincoln-Douglas Debates*, 131.
36. Whig editor Thurlow Weed prepared a pamphlet for the 1840 campaign that contained lengthy extracts from the 1821 Constitutional Convention. *Votes and Speeches of Martin Van Buren, on the Subjects of the Right of Suffrage, the Qualifications of Coloured Persons to Vote, and the Appointment or Election of Justices of the Peace* (Albany, NY: printed by the editor, 1840).
37. Lincoln to Richard F. Barrett, April 17, 1840, *Collected Works*, 1:209.
38. See, e.g., "Mr. Van Buren in the New York Convention," *Sangamo Journal*, July 10, 1840, 2; "Martin Van Buren for Free Negro Suffrage," *Sangamo Journal*, July 10, 1840, 1; "Martin Van Buren opposed to Universal Suffrage," *Sangamo Journal*, July 10, 1840, 1.
39. Lincoln, "Speech at Tremont, Illinois," May 2, 1840, *Collected Works*, 1:209–10.
40. Wilson and Davis, *Herndon's Informants*, 471; William M. Holland, *The Life and Political Opinions of Martin Van Buren, Vice President of the United States* (Hartford, CT: Belknap and Hamersley, 1835); "Facts in 'the Life of Martin Van Buren,'" *Sangamo Journal*, April 24, 1840, 2; "Martin Van Buren's endorsement of 'Holland's Life of Van Buren,'" *Sangamo Journal*, September 18, 1840, 2; Robert W. Johannsen, *Stephen A. Douglas* (Urbana: University of Illinois Press), 79–80.
41. See, e.g., "Mr. Van Buren's Negro Witnesses," *Sangamo Journal*, July 17, 1840, 2.
42. Williamson, *American Suffrage*, 117–37, 184.
43. Christopher Collier, "The American People as Christian White Men of Property: Suffrage and Elections in Colonial and Early National America," in *Voting and the Spirit of American Democracy: Essays on the History of Voting and Voting Rights in America*, ed. Donald W. Rogers (Urbana: University of Illinois Press, 1992), 26.
44. Illinois Constitution of 1818, art. 2, sec. 27.

45. An Act to Incorporate the City of Chicago, sec. 9, March 4, 1837, *Laws of the State of Illinois Passed at the Tenth General Assembly* (Vandalia, IL: William Walters, 1837), 52.
46. An Act to Incorporate the City of Springfield, art. 4, February 3, 1840, *Laws of the State of Illinois Passed at the Eleventh General Assembly* (Springfield, IL: William Walters, 1840), 8.
47. "To the Editor of the Journal," *Sangamo Journal*, June 25, 1836, 2.
48. "To the Voters of Sangamon County," *Sangamo Journal*, June 25, 1836, 2.
49. "To the Voters of Sangamon County," *Sangamo Journal*, July 2, 1836, 2.
50. Thomas Jefferson to Samuel Kercheval, July 12, 1816, in *The Essential Jefferson*, ed. Jean M. Yarbrough (Indianapolis: Hackett Publishing, 2006), 241; Sean Wilentz, *The Rise of American Democracy: Jefferson to Lincoln* (New York: W. W. Norton, 2005), 199–201.
51. Bruce Levine, "'The Vital Element of the Republican Party': Antislavery, Nativism, and Abraham Lincoln," *Journal of the Civil War Era* 1 (December 2011): 502n43.
52. Wilentz, *Rise of American Democracy*, 482–84.
53. "Theory of Political Representation," *American Quarterly Review* 20 (September 1836): 208.
54. Wilentz, *Rise of American Democracy*, 309–10.
55. On military service and citizenship in antebellum America, see Ricardo A. Herrera, *For Liberty and the Republic: The American Citizen as Soldier, 1775–1861* (New York: New York University Press, 2015).
56. Harry E. Pratt, "Lincoln in the Black Hawk War," *Bulletin of the Abraham Lincoln Association*, no. 54 (December 1938): 1, 4–13; Kenneth J. Winkle, *The Young Eagle: The Rise of Abraham Lincoln* (Dallas: Taylor Trade Publishing, 2001), 86–95.
57. Lincoln, "Autobiography Written for John L. Scripps," [ca. June 1860], *Collected Works*, 4:64.
58. Lincoln, "Brief Autobiography," June 1858, *Collected Works*, 2:459; Lincoln to Jesse W. Fell, December 20, 1859, *Collected Works*, 3:512; Lincoln, "Autobiography Written for John L. Scripps," *Collected Works*, 4:64.
59. Lincoln to Jesse W. Fell, 3:512. On the importance of the Black Hawk War for launching political careers, see Douglas L. Wilson, *Honor's Voice: The Transformation of Abraham Lincoln* (New York: Alfred A. Knopf, 1998), 49.
60. *Sangamo Journal*, July 19, 1832, 3.
61. Keyssar, *Right to Vote*, 27–28.
62. An Act to Provide for Raising a Revenue, March 1, 1827, sec. 17, *Revised Laws of Illinois* (Vandalia, IL: Greiner and Sherman 1833), 517; also see

An Act Amending the Act Providing for the Establishment of Free Schools, February 17, 1827, sec. 4, *Revised Laws*, 555.

63. John Mack Faragher, *Sugar Creek: Life on the Illinois Prairie* (New Haven, CT: Yale University Press, 1986), 106–7.
64. Daniel W. Stowell, "*Femes* Un*Covert:* Women's Encounters with the Law," in *In Tender Consideration: Women, Families, and the Law in Lincoln's Illinois*, ed. Daniel W. Stowell (Urbana: University of Illinois Press 2002), 17–45.
65. Stacy Pratt McDermott, "Dissolving the Bonds of Matrimony: Women and Divorce in Sangamon County, Illinois, 1837–1860," in *In Tender Consideration*, 84.
66. On Lincoln and Blackstone, see Mark E. Steiner, "Abraham Lincoln and the Rule of Law Books," *Marquette Law Review* 93 (Summer 2010): 1298, 1302–9.
67. William Blackstone, *Commentaries on the Laws of England* (New York: W. E. Dean, 1832), 1:355, 365; Linda K. Kerber, "From the Declaration of Independence to the Declaration of Sentiments: The Legal Status of Women in the Early Republic, 1776–1848," *Human Rights* 6 (Winter 1977): 118–19.
68. Corrine T. Field, *The Struggle for Equal Adulthood: Gender, Race, Age, and the Fight for Citizenship in Antebellum America* (Chapel Hill: University of North Carolina Press, 2014), 59.
69. William H. Herndon to Jesse W. Weik, February 11, 1887, in William H. Herndon, *Herndon on Lincoln: Letters*, ed. Douglas L. Wilson and Rodney O. Davis (Urbana: University of Illinois Press, 2016), 234.
70. William H. Herndon to John C. Henderson, [1886–1887?], in Herndon, *Herndon on Lincoln*, 346.
71. Burlingame, *Abraham Lincoln*, 1:104. Burlingame cites a story written by the woman's granddaughter eighty years later. Helen Ruth Reed, "A Prophecy Lincoln Made," *Boston Herald*, February 9, 1930.
72. Wilson, *Honor's Voice*, 69–71; Fern Nance Pond, *Intellectual New Salem in Lincoln's Day* (Harrogate, TN: Lincoln Memorial University, 1938), 16–17. Although Pond had access to the minutes of several literary societies, those records no longer appear to be extant. Pond's notes on the minutes are located at the Menard County Historical Society. These notes are a little more detailed than Pond's address on intellectual New Salem. Tyro-Polemic & Literary Club notes, Fern Nance Pond Papers, Menard County Historical Society. I thank Lois J. Adams of the Menard County Historical Society for scanning the notes for me.
73. Thomas F. Schwartz, "The Springfield Lyceums and Lincoln's 1838 Speech," *Illinois Historical Journal* 83 (Spring 1990): 45–49.

74. On colonization, see *Sangamo Journal*, December 21, 1833, 3; on phrenology, see *Sangamo Journal*, April 4, 1835, 3; on capital punishment, see *Sangamo Journal*, February 6, 1836, 2.
75. Frederick Douglass, "The Rights of Women," *North Star*, July 28, 1848, reprinted in Philip S. Foner, ed., *The Life and Writings of Frederick Douglass*, vol. 1, *Early Years, 1817–1849* (New York: International Publishers, 1950), 320–21; Benjamin Quarles, "Frederick Douglass and the Woman's Rights Movement," *Journal of Negro History* 25 (January 1940): 35–44; Wendell Phillips, "Capital Punishment—Women's Rights," *Liberator*, July 3, 1846, 3; "Woman's Rights Convention; Has Woman a Right to Vote? Speeches by Mrs. Wright, Miss Susan B. Anthony, Wendell Phillips, Ernestine L. Ross, Rev. Beriah Green, Elizabeth Johnes and Others. What Is Woman's Sphere?," *New York Times*, May 11, 1860, 8.
76. "Theory of Political Representation," *American Quarterly Review*, 201.
77. Ellen Carol DuBois, *Woman Suffrage and Women's Rights* (New York: New York University Press, 1998), 31, 38.
78. Lori D. Ginzberg, *Untidy Origins: A Story of Woman's Rights in Antebellum New York* (Chapel Hill: University of North Carolina 2005), 5–6.
79. Elizabeth Cady Stanton, Susan B. Anthony, and Matilda Joslyn Gage, eds., *History of Woman Suffrage*, vol. 1, *1848–1861* (New York: Arno Press, 1969), 73; Sue Davis, *The Political Thought of Elizabeth Cady Stanton: Women's Rights and the American Political Traditions* (New York: New York University Press, 2008), 56–57; Elisabeth Griffith, *In Her Own Right: The Life of Elizabeth Cady Stanton* (New York: Oxford University Press, 1984), 55.
80. Douglass, "Rights of Women," 3; Frederick Douglass, *Life and Times of Frederick Douglass, Written by Himself* (Hartford, CT: Park Publishing, 1882), 574–76; David W. Blight, *Frederick Douglass: Prophet of Freedom* (New York: Simon and Schuster, 2018), 196–97; Sally G. McMillen, *Seneca Falls and the Origins of the Women's Rights Movement* (New York: Oxford University Press, 2008), 93–94.
81. Samuel Jones, *Treatise on the Right of Suffrage* (Boston: Otis, Broaders, 1842), 152–55.
82. Laura E. Free, *Suffrage Reconstructed: Gender, Race, and Voting Rights in the Civil War Era* (Ithaca, NY: Cornell University Press, 2015), 21–23.
83. *Illinois Journal* (Springfield), August 9, 1848, 4.
84. *Illinois Daily Journal* (Springfield), October 26, 1850, 3.
85. Judith Wellman, *The Road to Seneca Falls: Elizabeth Cady Stanton and the First Woman's Rights Convention* (Urbana: University of Illinois Press, 2004), 144.
86. Robert Bray, *Reading with Lincoln* (Carbondale: Southern Illinois University Press, 2010), 41–81.

87. Mary Wollstonecraft, *A Vindication of the Rights of Woman* (Boston: Peter Edes, 1792).
88. Wilson, *Honor's Voice*, 85.
89. Lincoln, "Address before the Young Men's Lyceum of Springfield, Illinois," January 27, 1838, *Collected Works*, 1:115.
90. Wilson and Davis, *Herndon's Informants*, 441 (interview with Isaac Cogdal).
91. Morton J. Horwitz, "Treatise Literature," *Law Library Journal* 69 (November 1976): 460.
92. Wilson, *Honor's Voice*, 213–14.
93. Elizabeth R. Varon, *We Mean to Be Counted: White Women and Politics in Antebellum Virginia* (Chapel Hill: University of North Carolina Press, 1998), 71–72, 80.
94. Varon, *We Mean to Be Counted*, 75–76.
95. *Sangamo Journal*, October 16, 1840, 2.
96. "Great Meeting in Macoupin," *Sangamo Journal*, July 31, 1840, 2; "Log Cabin Raising," *Sangamo Journal*, November 6, 1840, 2.
97. "Young Men's State Convention," *Sangamo Journal*, June 5, 1840, 3.
98. James C. Conkling to fiancée Mercy Levering, as quoted in Paul M. Angle, *"Here I Have Lived": A History of Lincoln's Springfield, 1821–1865* (Springfield, IL: Abraham Lincoln Association, 1935), 115.
99. Wilson, *Honor's Voice*, 220.
100. Wilson, *Honor's Voice*, 215.
101. Jean H. Baker, *Mary Todd Lincoln: A Biography* (New York: W. W. Norton, 1987), 85–86, 94, 180–81.
102. Lincoln, "Letter from the Lost Townships," August 27, 1842, *Collected Works*, 1:295.
103. Baker, *Mary Todd Lincoln*, 133–34.
104. Miller, *Lincoln and His World*, 75.

2. Lincoln Knew Something

1. An Act to establish a uniform rule of Naturalization, and to repeal the acts heretofore passed on that subject, April 14, 1802, ch. 28, *U.S. Statutes at Large* 2 (1850), 153–54.
2. Erika Lee, *America for Americans: A History of Xenophobia in the United States* (New York: Basic Books, 2019), 39–73.
3. Keyssar, *Right to Vote*, 53, 67–68.
4. G. S. Boritt, *Lincoln and the Economics of the American Dream* (Memphis, TN: Memphis State University Press, 1978), 27, 98.
5. Lincoln, "Speech and Resolutions concerning Philadelphia Riots," June 12, 1844, *Collected Works*, 1:337–38.
6. Tyler Anbinder, *Nativism and Slavery: The Northern Know Nothings and the Politics of the 1850s* (New York: Oxford University Press, 1994), 11.

7. Lincoln, "Speech and Resolutions concerning Philadelphia Riots," 1:338.
8. "Illinois Mass Convention at Vandalia, July 17, 1844," *Sangamo Journal*, August 8, 1844, 3.
9. Kenneth J. Winkle, "The Second Party System in Lincoln's Springfield," *Civil War History* 44 (1998), 281–82.
10. Johannsen, *Stephen A. Douglas*, 67–69; Charles Manfred Thompson, "The Illinois Whigs before 1846," *University of Illinois Studies in the Social Sciences* 4 (1915), 79–80.
11. Lincoln to John T. Stuart, January 1, 1840, *Collected Works*, 1:181.
12. "Foreign Voters," *Sangamo Journal*, September 1, 1838, 2.
13. Keyssar, *Right to Vote*, 65.
14. "To the Editor of the *Chicago American*," June 24, 1839, *Collected Works*, 1:151.
15. "Illinois Election," *Sangamo Journal*, August 25, 1838, 2; see also "The Belleville Representative," *Sangamo Journal*, February 23, 1839, 2.
16. "Stuart and Douglass," *Sangamo Journal*, December 15, 1838, 2.
17. "Important Decision," *Sangamo Journal*, November 29, 1839, 2; "The 'Alien Case,'" *Sangamo Journal*, December 17, 1839, 2; "The Alien Case—No. II," *Sangamo Journal*, December 27, 1839, 2.
18. Thomas Ford, *A History of Illinois* (1854: repr., Urbana: University of Illinois Press, 1995), 146–53; Johannsen, *Stephen A. Douglas*, 82–87.
19. Spragins v. Houghton, 3 Illinois Reports 377, 414 (1840) (opinion by Justice Smith).
20. Miller, *Lincoln and His World*, 419–20.
21. Miller, *Lincoln and His World*, 420–25.
22. I ran a search for "Judge Douglas" in the online version of Lincoln's *Collected Works*, which resulted in 738 matches. *Collected Works of Abraham Lincoln*, available at https://quod.lib.umich.edu/l/lincoln/.
23. Miller, *Lincoln and His World*, 380.
24. An Act to Incorporate the City of Alton, July 21, 1837, *Laws of the State of Illinois, Passed by the Tenth General Assembly, at their Special Session* (Vandalia, IL: William Walters, 1837), 19; see also An Act to Incorporate the City of Chicago, March 4, 1837, *Laws of the State of Illinois, Passed by the Tenth General Assembly* (Vandalia, IL: William Walters, 1837), 52.
25. Winkle, "Second Party System in Lincoln's Springfield," 267, 272–73; An Act to Incorporate the City of Springfield, February 3, 1840, *Laws of the State of Illinois, Passed by the Eleventh General Assembly* (Springfield, IL: William Walters, 1840), 8–9.
26. Harry Pratt, "Lincoln—Trustee of the Town of Springfield," *Bulletin of the Abraham Lincoln Association*, no. 48 (June 1937): 6.
27. Pratt, "Lincoln," 6.
28. "City of Springfield," *Sangamo Journal*, April 10, 1840, 2.

29. An Act to Amend "An Act to Incorporate the City of Springfield," February 27, 1841, *Laws of the State of Illinois, Passed by the Twelfth General Assembly* (Springfield, IL: Wm. Walters, 1841), 61–62.
30. Frank Cicero Jr., *Creating the Land of Lincoln: The History and Constitutions of Illinois, 1778–1870* (Urbana: University of Illinois Press, 2018), 115–18, 121–24.
31. On Native American justifications for the Philadelphia riots, see *Important Testimony Connected with Native American Principles* (Philadelphia: First District Native American Association, 1845); John Hancock Lee, *The Origin and Progress of the American Party in Politics* (Philadelphia: Elliott and Gihon, 1855).
32. Anbinder, *Nativism and Slavery*, 9–14; Michael F. Holt, *The Rise and Fall of the American Whig Party: Jacksonian Politics and the Onset of the Civil War* (New York: Oxford University Press, 1999), 190–91.
33. Arthur Charles Cole, ed., *The Constitutional Debates of 1847* (Springfield: Illinois State Historical Library, 1919), 527.
34. Cole, *Constitutional Debates of 1847*, 534.
35. Cole, *Constitutional Debates of 1847*, 526 (statement of William C. Kinney).
36. Cole, *Constitutional Debates of 1847*, 517–18.
37. See, e.g., Cole, *Constitutional Debates of 1847*, 541 (statement of William R. Archer), 552 (statement of Thompson Campbell).
38. Illinois Constitution of 1848, art. 6, sec. 1.
39. Lincoln, "Opinion on Election Laws," November 1, 1852, *Collected Works*, 2:160.
40. Holt, *Rise and Fall of the American Whig Party*, 691–97; Wilentz, *Rise of American Democracy*, 679–85; Lincoln, "Speech to the Springfield Scott Club," August 14, 1852, *Collected Works*, 2:143.
41. Stephen E. Maizlish, "The Meaning of Nativism and the Crisis of the Union: The Know-Nothing Movement in the Antebellum North," in *Essays on Antebellum Politics 1840–1860*, ed. Stephen E. Maizlish and John J. Kushma (College Station: Texas A&M University Press, 1982), 170.
42. John P. Senning, "The Know Nothing Movement in Illinois, 1854–1856," *Journal of the Illinois State Historical Society* 7 (April 1914): 9, 27–29.
43. Senning, "Know Nothing Movement in Illinois," 17.
44. David Davis to Lincoln, December 26, 1854, Abraham Lincoln Papers, Library of Congress.
45. Lincoln to Jesse W. Fell, December 20, 1859, *Collected Works*, 3:512.
46. Senning, "Know-Nothing Movement in Illinois," 19.
47. N[oah] Levering, "Recollections of Abraham Lincoln," *Iowa Historical Record* 12 (July 1896): 495–97; Don E. Fehrenbacher and Virginia Fehrenbacher, eds., *Recollected Words of Abraham Lincoln* (Stanford, CA: Stanford University Press, 1996), lii–liii, 20–21.

48. Levering, "Recollections of Abraham Lincoln," 497.
49. See, generally, Jason H. Silverman, *Lincoln and the Immigrant* (Carbondale: Southern Illinois University Press, 2015).
50. Wilson, *Honor's Voice*, 7, 81–83, 187; Richard N. Current, *The Lincoln Nobody Knows* (New York: Hill and Wang, 1958), 51–65.
51. Matthew Pinsker, "Not Always Such a Whig: Abraham Lincoln's Partisan Realignment in the 1850s," *Journal of the Abraham Lincoln Association* 29 (Summer 2008), 34–38.
52. Lincoln, "Speech at Springfield," September 9, 1854, *Collected Works*, 2:229.
53. Lincoln, "Speech at Bloomington," September 26, 1854, *Collected Works*, 2:234.
54. Arthur Charles Cole, *The Centennial History of Illinois*, vol. 3, *The Era of the Civil War, 1848–1870* (Springfield: Illinois Centennial Commission, 1919), 133–34.
55. Matthew Pinsker, "Senator Abraham Lincoln," *Journal of the Abraham Lincoln Association* 14 (Summer 1993): 1–21.
56. Donald, *Lincoln*, 181–85; Holt, *Rise and Fall of the American Whig Party*, 870–71.
57. Lincoln to Owen Lovejoy, August 11, 1855, *Collected Works*, 2:316–17.
58. Lincoln to Joshua F. Speed, August 24, 1855, *Collected Works*, 2:323.
59. "Platform of Principles," *Chicago Daily Tribune*, February 9, 1856, 1.
60. Theodor Canisius, *Abraham Lincoln: Historisches Charakterbild* (Vienna: Reisser, 1867), quoted and translated in Frank Baron, "Abraham Lincoln and the German Immigrants: Turners and Forty-Eighters," *Yearbook of German-American Studies* 4, supplemental issue (2012): 85.
61. Burlingame, *Abraham Lincoln*, 1:412–13.
62. Green Berry Raum, *History of Illinois Republicanism* (Chicago: Rollins Publishing, 1900), 28.
63. Thomas F. Schwartz, "Lincoln, Form Letters, and Fillmore Men," *Illinois Historical Journal* 78 (Spring 1985): 65–70.
64. Lincoln, "Editorial on the Right of Foreigners to Vote," July 23, 1856, *Collected Works*, 2:355–56.
65. Eric Foner, *Free Soil, Free Labor, Free Men: The Ideology of the Republican Party before the Civil War* (1970; repr., New York: Oxford University Press, 1995), 250–60; Levine, "Vital Element of the Republican Party."
66. Stephen A. Douglas to John A. McClernand, December 23, 1856, quoted in Stephen Hansen and Paul Nygard, "Stephen A. Douglas, the Know-Nothings, and the Democratic Party in Illinois, 1854–1858," *Illinois Historical Journal* 87 (Summer 1994): 121–22.
67. Lincoln, "Speech at Chicago," July 10, 1858, *Collected Works*, 2:499–500.
68. Davis and Wilson, *Lincoln-Douglas Debates*, 282.
69. Lincoln, "Speech at Chicago," 2:499–500.

70. Lincoln, "Second Lecture on Discoveries and Inventions," February 11, 1859, *Collected Works*, 3:358.
71. Davis and Wilson, *Lincoln-Douglas Debates*, 202.
72. Charles J. McClain, *In Search of Equality: The Chinese Struggle against Discrimination in Nineteenth-Century America* (Berkeley: University of California Press, 1994), 9–23.
73. Treaty of Peace, Friendship, Limits, and Settlement with the Republic of Mexico, February 2, 1848, *U.S. Statutes at Large* 9 (1851), 929.
74. Steven Johnston, *Lincoln: The Ambiguous Icon* (Lanham, MD: Rowan and Littlefield, 2018), 149–73.
75. David A. Nichols, *Lincoln and the Indians: Civil War Policy and Politics* (St. Paul: Minnesota Historical Society Press, 2012), 186–89.
76. Lincoln, "Speech to Indians," March 27, 1863, *Collected Works*, 6:151–52.
77. Lincoln, "Annual Message to Congress," December 8, 1863, *Collected Works*, 7:47–48.
78. Stephen Kantrowitz, "White Supremacy, Settler Colonialism, and the Two Citizenships of the Fourteenth Amendment," *Journal of the Civil War Era* 10 (March 2020): 29–53.
79. Silverman, *Lincoln and the Immigrant*, 36–40; "Abraham Lincoln. A Talk with the Late President's Law Partner," *New-York Tribune*, February 15, 1867, 2.
80. James M. Bergquist, "People and Politics in Transition: The Illinois Germans, 1850–1860," in *Ethnic Voters and the Election of Lincoln*, ed. Frederick C. Luebke (Lincoln: University of Nebraska Press, 1971), 196–97; Theodore Calvin Pease, *The Centennial History of Illinois*, vol. 2, *The Frontier State, 1818–1848* (Urbana: University of Illinois Press, 1987), 393.
81. Thomas J. McCormack, ed., *Memoirs of Gustave Koerner, 1809–1896*, 2 vols. (Cedar Rapids, IA: Torch Press, 1909), 2:32–33; Stuart Berg Flexner, *I Hear America Talking: An Illustrated Treasury of American Words and Phrases* (New York: Simon and Schuster, 1979), 130–31.
82. Alison Clark Efford, *German Immigrants, Race, and Citizenship in the Civil War Era* (New York: Cambridge University Press, 2013), 2, 69.
83. Lincoln to Gustave P. Koerner, July 15, 1858, *Collected Works*, 2:502; Lincoln to Gustave P. Koerner, August 6, 1858, *Collected Works*, 2:536–37; Abraham Lincoln to Norman B. Judd, September 23, 1858, *Collected Works*, 3:202; Lincoln to Gustave P. Koerner, July 25, 1858, *Collected Works*, 2:524.
84. Lincoln, "Speech to the Springfield Scott Club," August 14, 1852, *Collected Works*, 2:143.
85. Lincoln to Norman B. Judd, September 23, 1858, *Collected Works*, 3:202; see also Lincoln to Norman B. Judd, October 24, 1858, *Collected Works*, 3:330.

86. "Speech at Meredosia, Illinois," October 18, 1858, *Collected Works*, 3:328–29.
87. Anbinder, *Nativism and Slavery*, 247–53; Foner, *Free Soil*, 250–52.
88. Lincoln to Theodore Canisius, May 17, 1859, *Collected Works*, 3:380.
89. Lincoln to Theodore Canisius, May 17, 1859; "Mr. Lincoln on the Massachusetts Amendment," *Illinois State Journal* (Springfield), May 25, 1859, 1.
90. Lincoln to Schuyler Colfax, July 6, 1859, *Collected Works*, 3:390–91.
91. Contract with Theodore Canisius, May 30, 1859, *Collected Works*, 3:383.
92. *A Political Text-Book for 1860* (New York: Tribune Association, 1860), 26–27.
93. McCormack, *Memoirs of Gustave Koerner*, 2:89–90.
94. *Rail Splitter* (Chicago), June 23, 1860, 1.
95. "Coming by Thousands" and "The Irish Vote," *Freeport (IL) Wide Awake*, November 3, 1860, 1.
96. See, e.g., "Mr. Lincoln on Naturalization and Fusion," *Chicago Tribune*, May 26, 1860, 1; "Mr. Lincoln on Naturalization and Fusion," *Wisconsin State Journal* (Madison), May 28, 1860, 2.
97. Lincoln, "Speech to Germans at Cincinnati, Ohio," 4:202.

3. A White Man's Republic

1. V. Jacque Voegeli, *Free but Not Equal: The Midwest and the Negro during the Civil War* (Chicago: University of Chicago Press, 1967).
2. "The Illinois Slave Law," *Frederick Douglass' Paper*, September 2, 1853, 1.
3. See, generally, Elmer Gertz, "The Black Laws of Illinois," *Journal of the Illinois State Historical Society* 56 (Autumn 1963): 454–73; Paul Finkelman, "Slavery, the 'More Perfect Union,' and the Prairie State," *Illinois Historical Journal* 80 (Winter 1987): 248–69.
4. Campbell Gibson and Kay Jung, "Historical Census Statistics on Population Totals by Race, 1790 to 1990" (working paper no. 56, Population Division, US Census Bureau Washington, DC, September 2002).
5. Richard E. Hart, "Springfield's African Americans as a Part of the Lincoln Community," *Journal of the Abraham Lincoln Association* 20 (Winter 1999): 35.
6. Davis and Wilson, *Lincoln-Douglas Debates*, 189.
7. Wendell Phillips, *Speeches, Lectures, and Letters* (Boston: James Redpath, 1863), 302.
8. "Speech of H. Ford Douglass [*sic*]," *Liberator*, July 13, 1860, 1; on Douglas, see, generally, Matthew Norman, "The Other Lincoln-Douglas Debate: The Race Issue in a Comparative Context," *Journal of the Abraham Lincoln Association* 31 (Winter 2010): 1–21; Robert L. Harris Jr., "H. Ford

Douglas: Afro-American Antislavery Emigrationist," *Journal of Negro History*, 62 (July 1977): 217–34.

9. "Speech of H. Ford Douglass," *Liberator*, 1.
10. "Speech of H. Ford Douglass [*sic*]," *Anti-Slavery Bugle* (Salem, OH), October 6, 1860, 2.
11. "Speech of H. Ford Douglass," *Liberator*, 1.
12. "Speech of H. Ford Douglass," *Liberator*, 1.
13. "Speech of H. Ford Douglass," *Anti-Slavery Bugle*, 2.
14. Foner, *Free Soil*, 286.
15. "Speech of H. Ford Douglass," *Liberator*, 1.
16. Lincoln, "Speech at Columbus, Ohio," September 16, 1859, *Collected Works*, 3:401.
17. "Speech of H. Ford Douglass," *Liberator*, 1; Lincoln, "Speech at Columbus, Ohio," 3:401–3. See also Harry V. Jaffa and Robert W. Johannsen, eds., *In the Name of the People: Speeches and Writings of Lincoln and Douglas in the Ohio Campaign of 1859* (Columbus: Ohio State University Press, 1959), 48–50.
18. "Speech of H. Ford Douglass," *Liberator*, 1.
19. Paul Finkelman, "Slavery and the Northwest Ordinance: A Study in Ambiguity," *Journal of the Early Republic* 6 (Winter 1986): 343–70.
20. Finkelman, "Slavery, the 'More Perfect Union,' and the Prairie State" 250.
21. Paul Finkelman, "Evading the Ordinance: The Persistence of Bondage in Indiana and Illinois," *Journal of the Early Republic* 9 (Spring 1989): 22, 41–42.
22. An Act to prevent the Migration of free Negroes and Mullattoes into this Territory and for other purposes, December 8, 1813, reprinted in Francis S. Philbrick, ed., *The Laws of Illinois Territory 1809–1818*, Collections of the Illinois State Historical Library (Springfield: Illinois State Historical Library, 1950), 25:91–92.
23. An Act Concerning Negroes and Mullattoes, December 22, 1814, reprinted in *Laws of Illinois Territory*, 157–58.
24. Illinois Constitution of 1818, art. 6; Cicero, *Creating the Land of Lincoln*, 55–60.
25. An Act respecting free Negroes, Mulattoes, Servants and Slaves, March 30, 1819, *Laws Passed by the First General Assembly of the State of Illinois* (Kaskaskia, IL: Blackwell and Berry, 1819), 354–56.
26. An Act respecting free Negroes, Mulattoes, Servants and Slaves, 360.
27. Leon F. Litwack, *North of Slavery: The Negro in the Free States, 1790–1860* (Chicago: University of Chicago Press, 1961), 93; Criminal Jurisprudence, Division 3, sec. 16, and ch. 40, Evidence and Depositions, sec. 23, *Revised Statutes, State of Illinois* (Springfield, IL: William Walters, 1845), 154, 237.

28. Lincoln, "Speech at Springfield, Illinois," June 26, 1857, *Collected Works*, 2:405; ch. 69, Marriages, sec. 2, ch. 74, Negroes, Mulattoes, &c, sec. 23, *Revised Statutes State of Illinois*, 353, 391.
29. Arthur Charles Cole, ed., *The Constitutional Debates of 1847* (Springfield: Illinois State Historical Library, 1919), 201–3.
30. Cole, *Constitutional Debates of 1847*, 201–3.
31. Cole, *Constitutional Debates of 1847*, 217, 227, 223, 228.
32. Cole, *Constitutional Debates of 1847*, 204.
33. Cole, *Constitutional Debates of 1847*, 213.
34. Jerome B. Meites, "The 1847 Illinois Constitutional Convention and Persons of Color," *Journal of the Illinois State Historical Society* 108 (Fall/Winter 2015): 282.
35. Meites, "1847 Illinois Constitutional Convention and Persons of Color," 284.
36. Winkle, *Young Eagle*, 261.
37. Litwack, *North of Slavery*, 70–71.
38. *General Laws of the State of Illinois Passed by the Eighteenth General Assembly* (Springfield, IL: Lanphier and Walker, 1853), 57–60; *Journal of the House of Representatives of the Eighteenth General Assembly of the State of Illinois* (Springfield, IL: Lanphier and Walker, 1853), 444.
39. Eugene H. Berwanger, *The Frontier against Slavery: Western Anti-Negro Prejudice and the Slavery Extension Controversy* (Urbana: University of Illinois Press, 1967), 49.
40. *Illinois Daily Journal*, March 1, 1853, 2.
41. *Illinois Daily Journal*, April 2, 1853, 2.
42. *Ottawa (IL) Free Trader*, Feb. 26, 1853, 2.
43. *Chicago Democratic Press* quoted in *Illinois Daily Journal*, March 1, 1853, 2.
44. *Frederick Douglass' Paper*, March 18, 1853, 2.
45. *Liberator*, April 1, 1853, 1.
46. Stephen Middleton, "The Judicial Construction of Whiteness in the Borderlands of the Northwest Territory, 1803–1860," in *Freedom's Conditions in the U.S.-Canadian Borderlands in the Age of Emancipation*, ed. Tony Allan Freyer (Durham, NC: Carolina Academic Press, 2011), 228.
47. Davis and Wilson, *Lincoln-Douglas Debates*, 20.
48. Oregon Constitution of 1857, art. 1, sec. 35; Litwack, *North of Slavery*, 93.
49. Rankin v. Lydia, 9 Kentucky Reports (2 A.K. Marsh) 461, 467–79 (1820). The attorneys general of the United States were inconsistent in deciding whether blacks were denizens. Hugh Legare, in 1843, decided that free people of color were not aliens but rather denizens. Roger Taney, in 1831, and Caleb Cushing, in 1856, decided otherwise. Litwack, *North of Slavery*, 51–54.

50. Martha S. Jones, *Birthright Citizens: A History of Race and Rights in Antebellum America* (New York: Cambridge University Press, 2018), 88.
51. An Act to protect all Persons in the United States, and furnish the Means of their Vindication, April 9, 1866, ch. 31, *U.S. Statutes at Large* 14 (1868), 27.
52. Brian Dirck, *Abraham Lincoln and White America* (Lawrence: University Press of Kansas, 2012), 49.
53. Office Fee Book [June 1847], case file L05636, *The Law Practice of Abraham Lincoln*, 2nd ed., www.lawpracticeofabrahamlincoln.org. Fleurville appears in Lincoln's pleadings as Florville. On Fleurville and Lincoln, see Gossie Harold Hudson, "William Florville: Lincoln's Barber and Friend," *Negro History Bulletin* 37 (August 1, 1974): 279–81; John E. Washington, *They Knew Lincoln* (New York: Oxford University Press, 2018), 183–202.
54. Fleurville v. Stockdale, Sangamon County Circuit Court, case file L03260, *Law Practice of Abraham Lincoln.*
55. Lincoln to C. R. Welles, September 27, 1852, *Collected Works*, 2:159; Decree, September 21, 1853, Florville v. Allin, McLean County Circuit Court, case file L01647, *Law Practice of Abraham Lincoln.*
56. Lincoln to Major W. Packard, February 10, 1860, *Collected Works*, 3:518.
57. Lincoln, "Speech at Peoria, Illinois," October 16, 1854, *Collected Works*, 2:255; see also Richard Striner, *Lincoln and Race* (Carbondale: Southern Illinois University Press, 2012), 8–13.
58. On Lincoln's support of colonization, see Phillip Shaw Paludan, "Lincoln and Colonization: Policy or Propaganda?," *Journal of the Abraham Lincoln Association* 25 (Winter 2004): 23–37; Michael Vorenberg, "Abraham Lincoln and the Politics of Black Colonization," *Journal of the Abraham Lincoln Association* 14 (Summer 1993): 23–45.
59. Lincoln, "Speech at Peoria," 2:256.
60. Lincoln, "Speech at Peoria," 2:256.
61. Eric Foner, "The Ideology of the Republican Party," in *The Birth of the Grand Old Party: The Republicans' First Generation*, ed. Robert Engs and Randall Miller (Philadelphia: University of Pennsylvania Press, 2002), 9–10.
62. Douglas and Wilson, *Lincoln-Douglas Debates*, 34.
63. Lincoln, "A Bill for Abolishing Slavery in the District of Columbia," January 1849, Abraham Lincoln Papers, Library of Congress.
64. Davis and Wilson, *Lincoln-Douglas Debates*, 48–49.
65. Paludan, "Lincoln and Colonization," 32.
66. Merton Lynn Dillon, "The Antislavery Movement in Illinois: 1824–1835," *Journal of the Illinois State Historical Society* 47 (Summer 1954): 149–66.
67. Eric Foner, *The Fiery Trial: Abraham Lincoln and American Slavery* (New York: W. W. Norton, 2011), 130; *Thirty-Seventh Annual Report*

of the American Colonization Society (Washington, DC: C. Alexander, 1854).

68. William Lloyd Garrison, *Thoughts on African Colonization* (Boston: Garrison and Knapp, 1832); Paul Goodman, *Of One Blood: Abolitionism and the Origins of Racial Equality* (Berkeley: University of California Press, 1998), 36–53; Ousmane K. Power-Greene, *Against Wind and Tide: The African American Struggle against the Colonization Movement* (New York: New York University Press, 2014), 46–62.
69. *Alton (IL) Observer*, July 13, 1837, 1.
70. "To the Editors of the Old Soldier," *Old Soldier* (Springfield, IL), March 14, 1840, 3.
71. Power-Greene, *Against Wind and Tide*; Winkle, *Young Eagle*, 255–56. Historians have estimated that about 25 percent of free blacks were favorably disposed toward emigration from the time of the founding of the American Colonization Society until the Civil War. Daniel Walker Howe, *What Hath God Wrought: The Transformation of America, 1815–1848* (New York: Oxford University Press, 2007), 263.
72. Manisha Sinha, *The Slave's Cause: A History of Abolition* (New Haven, CT: Yale University Press, 2016), 574–80.
73. See, e.g., "Evidence in Favor of Colonization," *Chicago Daily Tribune*, October 17, 1853, 2.
74. David Brion Davis, *The Problem of Slavery in the Age of Emancipation* (New York: Vintage Books, 2015), 162–66.
75. "Colonization Society," *Illinois Journal* (Springfield), October 25, 1848, 1.
76. Elder S. S. Ball, *Report on the Condition and Prospects of the Republic of Liberia* (Alton, IL: Telegraph Office, 1848), 8, 12.
77. Donald, *Lincoln*, 167.
78. *Daily Illinois State Journal* (Springfield), February 18, 1858, 3.
79. *Daily Illinois State Journal* (Springfield), February 18, 1858, 3.
80. Charles A. Gliozzo, "John Jones and the Black Convention Movement, 1848–1856," *Journal of Black Studies* 3 (December 1972), 233–35; Victoria L. Harrison, "We Are Here Assembled: Illinois Colored Conventions, 1853–1873," *Journal of the Illinois State Historical Society* 108 (Fall/Winter 2015): 326–29.
81. *Proceedings of the First Convention of the Colored Citizens of the State of Illinois, Convened at the City of Chicago, Thursday, Friday, and Saturday, October 6th, 7th and 8th, 1853*, reprinted in Philip S. Foner and George E. Walker, eds., *The Proceedings of the Black State Conventions 1840–1865*, 2 vols. (Philadelphia: Temple University Press, 1980), 2:60, 64. The anti-colonization resolutions were published in the *Chicago Tribune*. "Colored Convention Reports," *Chicago Daily Tribune*, October 11, 1853, 3.

82. "Meeting of the Colored Citizens," *Chicago Daily Press and Tribune*, August 16, 1858, 1.
83. *Sangamo Journal*, November 17, 1832, 3; see also "Colonization Society," *Sangamo Journal*, January 12, 1832, 2.
84. "Colonization Society," *Sangamo Journal*, August 31, 1833, 3.
85. "Colonization Meeting," *Sangamo Journal*, October 18, 1839, 3; "Communication," *Sangamo Journal*, August 23, 1839, 2.
86. "Sangamon Colonization Society," *Sangamo Journal*, March 12, 1846, 2.
87. Vorenberg, "Abraham Lincoln and the Politics of Black Colonization," 25.
88. Daniel Walker Howe, *The Political Culture of the American Whigs* (Chicago: University of Chicago Press, 1979), 136–37; James Brewer Stewart, "The Emergence of Racial Modernity and the Rise of the White North, 1790–1840," *Journal of the Early Republic* 18 (Summer 1998), 205–6.
89. Charles Maltby, *The Life and Public Services of Abraham Lincoln* (Stockton, CA: Daily Independent Steam Power Print, 1884), 32–33.
90. Winkle, *Young Eagle*, 225.
91. Allen C. Guelzo, "Come-Outers and Community Men: Abraham Lincoln and the Idea of Community in Nineteenth-Century America," *Journal of the Abraham Lincoln Association* 21 (Winter 2000): 19–20.
92. Power-Greene, *Against Wind and Tide*, 61.
93. "Colonization Society," *Sangamo Journal*, January 23, 1845, 3.
94. "Illinois Colonization Society," *Sangamo Journal*, December 18, 1845, 2.
95. "Circular of the State Colonization Society," *Sangamo Journal*, June 18, 1850, 2.
96. *Illinois Daily Journal*, August 30, 1853, 3.
97. "Colonization," *Illinois Daily Journal*, January 14, 1854, 2.
98. "Annual Meeting of the Illinois State Colonization Society," *Illinois Daily Journal*, January 2, 1855, 2; Lincoln, "Outline for Speech to the Colonization Society," [January 4, 1855], *Collected Works*, 2:298–99; *Sunday Morning Republican* (St. Louis), January 7, 1855, 2.
99. See, e.g., Lincoln, "Eulogy on Zachary Taylor," July 25, 1850, *Collected Works*, 2:83; Lincoln, "Speech to the Springfield Scott Club," August 14, 26, 1852, *Collected Works*, 2:135.
100. See, e.g., *Thirty-Eighth Annual Report of the American Colonization Society* (Washington, DC: C. Alexander, 1855), 11.
101. Lincoln, "Eulogy on Henry Clay," July 6, 1852, *Collected Works*, 2:130.
102. Lincoln undoubtedly was quoting Clay's 1827 speech from the 1843 two-volume collection of Clay's speeches. *Life and Speeches of Henry Clay*, 2 vols. (New York: Greeley and McElrath, 1843) 1:267–84.
103. Lincoln, "Eulogy on Henry Clay," 2:130.

104. Lincoln, "Eulogy on Henry Clay," 2:133.
105. Nicholas Guyatt, "'The Outskirts of Our Happiness': Race and the Lure of Colonization in the Early Republic," *Journal of American History* 95 (March 2009): 986–1011; Andrew Diemer, "'A Desire to Better Their Condition': European Immigration, African Colonization, and the Lure of Consensual Emancipation," in *New Directions in the Study of African American Recolonization*, ed. Beverly C. Tomek and Matthew J. Hetrick (Gainesville: University Press of Florida, 2017), 256.
106. Lincoln, "Speech at Springfield," June 26, 1857, *Collected Works*, 2:409.
107. Lincoln, "Speech at Springfield," July 17, 1858, *Collected Works*, 2:521.
108. Lincoln, "Speech at Edwardsville," September 11, 1858, *Collected Works*, 3:91.
109. Davis and Wilson, *Lincoln-Douglas Debates*, 274.
110. Wickliffe Kitchell to Lincoln, June 14, 1858, Papers of Abraham Lincoln, Library of Congress.
111. "Republican State Convention," *Alton (IL) Weekly Telegraph*, June 24, 1858, 1.
112. "The Views and Sentiments of Henry Clay and Abe Lincoln, on the Slavery Question," *Chicago Tribune*, October 26, 1858, 2; "The Views and Sentiments of Henry Clay and Abe Lincoln, on the Slavery Question," *Daily Illinois State Journal* (Springfield), November 1, 1858, 1.
113. "The Republican Creed," *Daily Illinois State Journal* (Springfield), July 26, 1858, 2.
114. "The Republican Party and Negro Colonization," *Anti-Slavery Bugle*, March 31, 1860, 2; "A Probable Plank in the Chicago Platform," *Anti-Slavery Bugle*, March 31, 1860, 2–3; *A Political Text-Book for 1860* (New York: Tribune Association 1860), 26–27; Douglas R. Egerton, *Year of Meteors: Stephen Douglas, Abraham Lincoln, and the Election That Brought on the Civil War* (New York: Bloomsbury Press, 2010); Foner, *Free Soil*, 276–79; Michael S. Green, *Lincoln and the Election of 1860* (Carbondale: Southern Illinois University Press, 2011); William C. Harris, *Lincoln's Rise to the Presidency* (Lawrence: University Press of Kansas, 2007), 205–6.
115. "Richard J. Hinton Interview with Abraham Lincoln," *For the People* 22 (Spring 2020): 5. *For the People* is the bulletin of the Abraham Lincoln Association.

4. *Dred Scott* and Black Citizenship

1. Dred Scott v. John F. A. Sandford, 60 United States Reports (19 Howard) 393 (1857).
2. Dred Scott v. John F. A. Sandford, 403–4.
3. Paul Finkelman, "*Scott v. Sandford:* The Court's Most Dreadful Case and How It Changed History," *Chicago-Kent Law Review* 82 (2007),

3, 37; Roger Taney, Opinion of the Court, Dred Scott v. John F. A. Sandford, 406.

4. Roger Taney, Opinion of the Court, 407, 411.
5. Dred Scott v. John F. A. Sandford, 407, 410.
6. See, generally, Lucas E. Morel, "The *Dred Scott* Dissents: McLean, Curtis, Lincoln, and the Public Mind," *Journal of Supreme Court History* 32 (2007): 133–51.
7. John McLean, dissenting opinion, Dred Scott v. John F. A. Sandford, 531, 533.
8. Benjamin Curtis, dissenting opinion, Dred Scott v. John F. A. Sandford, 572–573, 576.
9. Curtis, dissenting opinion, 581–82.
10. Curtis, dissenting opinion, 583.
11. Don E. Fehrenbacher, *The* Dred Scott *Case: Its Significance in American Law and* Politics (New York: Oxford University Press), 417–48.
12. Frederick Douglass, *Two Speeches by Frederick Douglass* (Rochester, NY: C. P. Dewey, 1857), 31.
13. Fehrenbacher, Dred Scott *Case*, 429.
14. John M. Rozett, "Racism and Republican Emergence in Illinois, 1848–1860: A Re-evaluation of Republican Negrophobia," *Civil War History* 22 (June 1976): 101, 103.
15. *Remarks of the Hon. Stephen A. Douglas on Kansas, Utah, and the Dred Scott Decision* (Chicago: Daily Times Book and Job Office, 1857); Lincoln, "Speech at Springfield," Illinois, June 26, 1857, *Collected Works*, 2:398–410.
16. *Remarks of the Hon. Stephen A. Douglas*, 7.
17. *Remarks of the Hon. Stephen A. Douglas*, 7–8.
18. *Remarks of the Hon. Stephen A. Douglas*, 7, 10–11.
19. Lincoln to Newton Deming and George P. Strong, May 25, 1857, *Collected Works*, second supplement:13.
20. On Lincoln's preparation, see James F. Simon, *Lincoln and Chief Justice Taney: Slavery, Secession, and the President's War Powers* (New York: Simon and Schuster 2006), 136; Ronald C. White Jr., *A. Lincoln: A Biography* (New York: Random House, 2009), 238.
21. Lincoln, "Speech at Springfield," 2:401.
22. Lincoln, "Speech at Springfield," 2:408.
23. Lincoln, "Speech at Springfield, 2:403.
24. Lincoln, "Speech at Springfield, 2:403.
25. Davis and Wilson, *Lincoln-Douglas Debates*, 219.
26. Donald, *Lincoln*, 142, 151.
27. Steiner, *Honest Calling*, 61–65, 148–54.
28. Herndon and Weik, *Herndon's Lincoln*, 210.
29. Fehrenbacher, Dred Scott *Case*, 345, 349, 359. Paul Finkelman has noted that Taney's novel argument on citizenship was based "entirely on race"

and used "a slanted and one-sided history of the founding period." Finkelman, "*Scott v. Sandford*," 37.

30. Lincoln, "Speech at Springfield," 2:404.
31. Lincoln, "Speech at Springfield," 2:405.
32. Lincoln, "Notes for Speech at Chicago, Illinois," February 28, 1857, *Collected Works*, 2:391.
33. Lincoln, "Speech at Springfield," 2:405, 407.
34. Stephen A. Douglas, "The Contest in Illinois," *United States Democratic Review*, August 1858, 140–42.
35. Roy P. Basler's edition of Lincoln's *Collected Works* reproduces eight speeches given in this period: Chicago, July 10, 1858; Springfield, July 17, 1858; Clinton, July 27, 1858; Monticello, July 29, 1858; Beardstown, August 12, 1858; Havana, August 14, 1858; Bath, August 16, 1858; Lewistown, August 17, 1858. See Lincoln, *Collected Works*, 2:484–502, 504–21, 525–27, 538, 547.
36. Lincoln, "Speech at Springfield," 2:519.
37. Lincoln, "Speech at Chicago, Illinois," July 10, 1858, *Collected Works*, 2:497.
38. Lincoln, "Speech at Lewiston, Illinois," August 17, 1858, *Collected Works*, 2:546.
39. Lincoln, "Speech at Monticello, Illinois," July 29, 1858, *Collected Works*, 2:527.
40. Lincoln, "Speech at Chicago, Illinois," July 10, 1858, *Collected Works*, 2:495-496.
41. Davis and Wilson, *Lincoln-Douglas Debates*, 14.
42. Davis and Wilson, *Lincoln-Douglas Debates*, 14–15.
43. Davis and Wilson, *Lincoln-Douglas Debates*, 18, 20.
44. Davis and Wilson, *Lincoln-Douglas Debates*, 24, 31.
45. Davis and Wilson, *Lincoln-Douglas Debates*, 20–21.
46. Davis and Wilson, *Lincoln-Douglas Debates*, 131.
47. Davis and Wilson, *Lincoln-Douglas Debates*, 131–32.
48. Davis and Wilson, *Lincoln-Douglas Debates*, 156–57.
49. Davis and Wilson, *Lincoln-Douglas Debates*, 162–63.
50. Davis and Wilson, *Lincoln-Douglas Debates*, 164.
51. Davis and Wilson, *Lincoln-Douglas Debates*, 204–5.
52. Davis and Wilson, *Lincoln-Douglas Debates*, 215–16, 247.
53. Davis and Wilson, *Lincoln-Douglas Debates*, 254–55, 266.
54. Davis and Wilson, *Lincoln-Douglas Debates*, 268–69.
55. Davis and Wilson, *Lincoln-Douglas Debates*, 268–69.
56. *Illinois State Register* (Springfield), August 7, 1858.
57. Davis and Wilson, *Lincoln-Douglas Debates*, 8, 62, 89, 156–57, 160, 230.
58. Davis and Wilson, *Lincoln-Douglas Debates*, 62, 89.
59. Davis and Wilson, *Lincoln-Douglas Debates*, 89.
60. Davis and Wilson, *Lincoln-Douglas Debates*, 156–57.

61. Lyman Trumbull to Lincoln, June 12, 1858, Abraham Lincoln Papers, Library of Congress.
62. John M. Palmer to Lincoln, July 19, 1858, Abraham Lincoln Papers, Library of Congress.
63. David Davis to Lincoln, August 3, 1858, Abraham Lincoln Papers, Library of Congress.
64. Owen Lovejoy to Lincoln, August 4, 1858, Abraham Lincoln Papers, Library of Congress.
65. Jediah F. Alexander to Lincoln, August 5, 1858, Abraham Lincoln Papers, Library of Congress.
66. Joseph Medill to Lincoln, [August 27, 1858], Abraham Lincoln Papers, Library of Congress.
67. Foner, *Free Soil*, 284–85, 290–91, 294; Foner, *Fiery Trial*, 84; Litwack, *North of Slavery*, 278; Benjamin Quarles, *Lincoln and the Negro* (New York: Oxford University Press, 1962), 82.
68. Foner, *Free Soil*, 23.
69. Lincoln, "Address before the Wisconsin State Agricultural Society," September 30, 1855, *Collected Works*, 3:478.
70. G. S. Boritt, "The Right to Rise," in *The Public and the Private Lincoln: Contemporary Perspectives*, ed. Cullom Davis et al. (Carbondale: Southern Illinois University Press, 1979), 57–70; Boritt, *Lincoln and the Economics of the American Dream*, 159–61.
71. Lincoln, "Address before the Wisconsin State Agricultural Society," 3:479.
72. Lincoln, "Speech at New Haven, Connecticut," March 6, 1860, *Collected Works*, 4:24–25.
73. Lincoln, "Address before the Wisconsin State Agricultural Society," 3:479.
74. Lincoln, "Speech at Indianapolis, Indiana," September 19, 1859, *Collected Works*, 3:469.
75. Lincoln, "Speech at Springfield, Illinois, June 26, 1857, *Collected Works*, 2:405.
76. Lincoln, "Speech at Springfield, Illinois," July 17, 1858, *Collected Works*, 2:520; Davis and Wilson, *Lincoln-Douglas Debates*, 21, 217.
77. Davis and Wilson, *Lincoln-Douglas Debates*, 274, 282.
78. Harold Holzer, *Lincoln at Cooper Union: The Speech That Made Abraham Lincoln President* (New York: Simon and Schuster, 2004), 175–205.
79. Burlingame, *Abraham Lincoln*, 1:588–590; Lincoln, "Speech at Hartford, Connecticut," March 5, 1860, *Collected Works*, 4:7.
80. Lincoln, "Speech at New Haven," 4:24–25.
81. Joanne Pope Melish, "The 'Condition' Debate and Racial Discourse in the Antebellum North," *Journal of the Early Republic* 19 (Winter 1999): 651–72.

82. Joan E. Cashin, "Black Families in the Old Northwest," *Journal of the Early Republic* 15 (Autumn 1995): 460.

5. Citizenship and the Civil War

1. Lincoln used the phrase *ultimate extinction* more than fifty times during his Senate race. See, for example, Lincoln, "Speech at Springfield, Illinois," July 17, 1858, *Collected Works*, 2:514–15.
2. James M. McPherson, "The Transformation of Abraham Lincoln," *New York Review of Books*, November 25, 2010.
3. Frederick Douglass, "What Shall Be Done with the Negro?," May 16, 1863, *New York Times*, 8.
4. An Act to confiscate Property used for Insurrectionary Purposes, August 6, 1861, ch. 60, *U.S. Statutes at Large* 12 (1863), 319. On the First Confiscation Act, see James Oakes, "Reluctant to Emancipate? Another Look at the First Confiscation Act," *Journal of the Civil War Era* 3 (December 2013): 458–66.
5. Lincoln, "Annual Message to Congress," December 3, 1861, *Collected Works*, 5:48.
6. Lincoln, "Annual Message to Congress," 5:48.
7. Robert E. May, *Slavery, Race, and Conquest in the Tropics: Lincoln, Douglas, and the Future of Latin America* (New York: Cambridge University Press, 2013), 265–67.
8. Lincoln to Caleb B. Smith, October [23?], 1861, *Collected Works*, 4:561; "Approval of Contract with Ambrose W. Thompson," September 11, 1862, *Collected Works*, 5:414; Paul J. Scheips, "Lincoln and the Chiriqui Colonization Project," *Journal of Negro History* 37 (October 1952): 419–20.
9. An Act for the Release of certain Persons held to Service or Labor in the District of Columbia, April 16, 1862, ch. 54, *U.S. Statutes at Large* 12 (1863), 376–78; Kate Masur, *An Example for All the Land: Emancipation and the Struggle for Equality in Washington, D.C.* (Chapel Hill: University of North Carolina Press, 2010), 24–29.
10. Burlingame, *Abraham Lincoln,* 2:286–92.
11. Lincoln, "Message to Congress," April 16, 1862, *Collected Works*, 5:192.
12. "The Colored People on Colonization," *Boston Herald*, April 30, 1862, 4.
13. US Congress, House of Representatives, Select Committee on Emancipation, Emancipation and Colonization (to Accompany H.R. 576), 37th Cong., 2d Sess., 1862, H.R. No. 148, 13, 15.
14. US Congress, House of Representatives, Select Committee on Emancipation, Emancipation and Colonization, 14.
15. US Congress, House of Representatives, Select Committee on Emancipation, Emancipation and Colonization, 16.

16. An Act making supplemental Appropriations for sundry Civil Expenses of the Government for the Year ending June thirtieth, eighteen hundred and sixty-three, and for the Year ending June thirtieth, eighteen hundred and sixty-two, and other purposes, July 16, 1862, ch. 182, *U.S. Statutes at Large* 12 (1863), 582–83.
17. Lincoln, "Appeal to Border State Representatives to Favor Compensated Emancipation," July 12, 1862, *Collected Works*, 5:318.
18. The definitive account of Lincoln's meeting with the delegation is Kate Masur, "The African American Delegation to Abraham Lincoln: A Reappraisal," *Civil War History* 56 (June 2010): 117–44.
19. Vorenberg, "Abraham Lincoln and the Politics of Black Colonization," 33; Mark E. Neely Jr., "Colonization and the Myth That Lincoln Prepared the People for Emancipation," in *Lincoln's Proclamation: Emancipation Reconsidered*, ed. William A. Blair and Karen Fisher Younger (Chapel Hill: University of North Carolina Press, 2009), 48; see also James Oakes, *Freedom National: The Destruction of Slavery in the United States, 1861–1865* (New York: W. W. Norton, 2013), 308–10.
20. Lincoln, "Address on Colonization to a Deputation of Negroes," August 14, 1862, *Collected Works*, 5:370–71.
21. "The President on Colonization," *Liberator*, August 29, 1862, 140.
22. Davis, *Problem of Slavery in the Age of Emancipation*, 83–166; George M. Fredrickson, *The Black Image in the White Mind: The Debate on Afro-American Character and Destiny, 1817–1914* (New York: Harper and Row, 1972), 1–27; Nicholas Guyatt, *Bind Us Apart: How Enlightened Americans Invented Racial Segregation* (New York: Basic Books, 2016), 247–80.
23. Lincoln, "Address on Colonization to a Deputation of Negroes," 5:370–71.
24. Lincoln, "Address on Colonization to a Deputation of Negroes," 5:372–73.
25. Lincoln, "Address on Colonization to a Deputation of Negroes," 5:372–73.
26. Lincoln, "Address on Colonization to a Deputation of Negroes," 5:374–75.
27. Edward M. Thomas to Lincoln, August 16, 1862, Abraham Lincoln Papers, Library of Congress.
28. Masur, "African American Delegation to Abraham Lincoln," 135–37.
29. *Baltimore Sun,* August 23, 1862, 4.
30. "The Colored Men's Response to the President," *Lowell (MA) Daily Citizen and News*, August 27, 1862, 2; "Central American Colonization," *Daily National Intelligencer* (Washington, DC), August 29, 1862, 3.
31. "Central American Colonization," *Daily National Intelligencer* (Washington, DC), 3; *Baltimore Sun,* August 22, 1862, 4; Masur, "African American Delegation to Abraham Lincoln," 138–39.

32. "The Colonization Scheme," *Daily National Intelligencer* (Washington, DC), August 27, 1862, 3.
33. "The President's Colonization Scheme," *National Republican* (Washington, DC), August 26, 1862, 2.
34. Scheips, "Lincoln and the Chiriqui Colonization Project," 435–37, 441.
35. "The Colored People of the District and Colonization," *Baltimore Sun*, November 5, 1862, 4.
36. Frederick Douglass, "The President and His Speeches," *Douglass' Monthly*, September 1862, 707.
37. Neely, "Colonization and the Myth," 49–51.
38. Robert Purvis, "Expatriation of the Colored Race," *New-York Daily Tribune*, September 20, 1862, 10; see also *An Appeal from the Colored Men of Philadelphia to the President of the United States* (Philadelphia: Semi-Weekly Clarion, 1862), 1–2, 5–6; "Reply to the President by the Colored People of Newtown, L.I.," *Lowell (MA) Daily Citizen and News,* September 16, 1862, 1.
39. David Donald, ed., *Inside Lincoln's Cabinet: The Civil War Diaries of Salmon P. Chase* (New York: Longmans, Green, 1954), 112.
40. Lincoln, "Preliminary Emancipation Proclamation," September 22, 1862, *Collected Works*, 5:434.
41. "Spirit of the Press," *Daily National Intelligencer* (Washington, DC), October 7, 1862, 2; "Spirit of the Press," *Daily National Intelligencer* (Washington, DC), October 8, 1862, 2; Louis P. Masur, *Lincoln's One Hundred Days: The Emancipation Proclamation and the War for the Union* (Cambridge, MA: Harvard University Press, 2012), 101–38; Lorraine A. Williams, "Northern Intellectual Reaction to the Policy of Emancipation," *Journal of Negro History* 46 (April 1961), 180–82.
42. Cincinnati Commercial editorial clipped in "Spirit of the Press," *Daily National Intelligencer* (Washington, DC), October 7, 1862, 2.
43. "The Colored People of Brooklyn upon the Proclamation and the Colonization of the Contrabands," *New York Times*, October 3, 1862, 2.
44. "The Hero of the Planter," *New York Times*, October 3, 1862, 8.
45. Thomas Schoonover, "Misconstrued Mission: Expansionism and Black Colonization in Mexico and Central America during the Civil War," *Pacific Historical Review* 49 (November 1980): 616–17; Mary Patrick Chapman, "The Mission of Elisha O. Crosby to Guatemala, 1861–1864," *Pacific Historical Review* 24 (August 1955): 278.
46. Nicholas Guyatt, "'The Future Empire of Our Freemen': Republican Colonization Schemes in Texas and Mexico, 1861–1865," in *Civil War Wests: Testing the Limits of the United States*, ed. Adam Arenson and Andrew R. Graybill (Oakland: University of California Press, 2015), 100–101.
47. Lincoln, "Annual Message to Congress," December 1, 1862, *Collected Works*, 5:520–21.

48. Lincoln, "Annual Message to Congress," 5:530.
49. Lincoln, "Annual Message to Congress," 5:534–36.
50. "The President's Message," *Weekly Anglo-African*, December 7, 1862, 2.
51. "Colonization," *New-York Daily Tribune*, February 24, 1862, 4.
52. *Opinion of Attorney General Bates on Citizenship* (Washington, DC: Government Printing Office, 1863), 3, 24–27.
53. "Citizenship of Colored Americans," *Douglass' Monthly* (February 1863), 797; Oakes, *Freedom National*, 359.
54. Salmon P. Chase to Lincoln, April 12, 1865, Abraham Lincoln Papers, Library of Congress; James P. McClure et al., "Circumventing the Dred Scott Decision: Edward Bates, Salmon P. Chase, and the Citizenship of African Americans," *Civil War History* 43 (December 1997): 280, 283.
55. *Opinion of Attorney General Bates on Citizenship*, 4–5.
56. "The Attorney-General on Citizenship," *New York Times*, December 27, 1862, 4.
57. Marvin R. Cain, *Lincoln's Attorney General: Edward Bates of Missouri* (Columbia: University of Missouri Press, 1965), 224–25.
58. James D. Lockett, "Abraham Lincoln and Colonization: An Episode That Ends in Tragedy at L'Ile à Vache, Haiti, 1863–1864," *Journal of Black Studies* 21 (June 1991): 428–44; William Seraille, "Afro-American Emigration to Haiti during the American Civil War," *The Americas* 35 (October 1978): 185–200.
59. Phillip W. Magness, "The Changing Legacy of Civil War Colonization," in *New Directions in the Study of African American Recolonization*, ed. Beverly C. Tomek and Matthew J. Hetrick (Gainesville: University Press of Florida, 2017), 305–6; see also Michael J. Douma, "The Lincoln Administration's Negotiations to Colonize African Americans in Dutch Suriname," *Civil War History* 61 (June 2015): 111–37.
60. Phillip W. Magness and Sebastian N. Page, *Colonization after Emancipation: Lincoln and the Movement for Black Resettlement* (Columbia: University of Missouri Press, 2011); Allen C. Guelzo, review of *Colonization after Emancipation: Lincoln and the Movement for Black Resettlement* by Phillip W. Magness and Sebastian N. Page, *Journal of the Abraham Lincoln Association* 34 (Winter 2013): 78–87.
61. See, e.g., "A Nice Colonization Plundering Scheme Exposed," *New York Herald*, March 17, 1864, 4; "The Colonization Humbug," *National Anti-Slavery Standard*, March 19, 1864, 3; "The Negro Colonies a Failure," *Cleveland Morning Leader*, March 22, 1864, 1; "Colonization Collapses," *New-York Daily Tribune*, March 22, 1864, 4.
62. "Colonization Humbug," *National Anti-Slavery Standard*, 3.
63. "The Crusade against Color," *Liberator*, April 8, 1864, 60.
64. An Act making Appropriations for sundry Civil Expenses of the Government, *U.S. Statutes at Large* 13 (1866), 352.

65. Michael Burlingame and John R. Turner Ettlinger, eds., *Inside Lincoln's White House: The Complete Civil War Diary of John Hay* (Carbondale: Southern Illinois University Press, 1999), 217.
66. Gabor Boritt, "Did He Dream of a Lily-White America? The Voyage to Linconia," in *The Lincoln Enigma: The Changing Faces of an American Icon*, ed. Gabor Boritt (New York: Oxford University Press, 2001), 13; James M. McPherson, *Battle Cry of Freedom: The Civil War Era* (New York: Oxford University Press, 1988), 508–9; James Oakes, *The Radical and the Republican: Frederick Douglass, Abraham Lincoln, and the Triumph of Antislavery Politics* (New York: W. W. Norton, 2007), 193–94.
67. Gideon Welles, "The History of Emancipation," *Galaxy* 14 (December 1872): 841–842; Cain, *Lincoln's Attorney General*, 219–22.
68. William E. Gienapp and Erica L. Gienapp, eds., *The Civil War Diaries of Gideon Welles, Lincoln's Secretary of the Navy: The Original Manuscript Edition* (Urbana: University of Illinois Press, 2014), 60.
69. "Benjamin F. Butler," in *Reminiscences of Abraham Lincoln by Distinguished Men of His Time*, ed. Allen Thorndike Rice (New York: North American Review, 1886), 139–60; Benjamin F. Butler, *Butler's Book: Autobiography and Personal Reminiscences of Major-General Benj. F. Butler* (Boston: A. M. Thayer, 1892), 902–9.
70. Mark E. Neeley Jr. wrote an influential takedown of Butler's testimony on Lincoln and colonization; more recently, Phillip W. Magness has tried to rehabilitate Butler. Magness does establish that the meeting between Lincoln and Butler could have occurred in April 1865. Mark E. Neeley Jr., "Abraham Lincoln and Black Colonization: Benjamin Butler's Spurious Testimony," *Civil War History* 25 (March 1979): 77–83; Phillip W. Magness, "Benjamin Butler's Colonization Testimony Reevaluated," *Journal of the Abraham Lincoln Association* 29 (Winter 2008): 1–28.
71. *Reminiscences of Abraham Lincoln by Distinguished Men of His Time*, 150–53.
72. Gienapp and Gienapp, *Civil War Diaries of Gideon Welles,* 69; Scheips, "Lincoln and the Chiriqui Colonization Project," 435–37, 441.
73. Neeley, "Abraham Lincoln and Black Colonization," 81; T. Harry Williams, *Lincoln and His Generals* (New York: Vintage Books, 1952), 215.
74. Butler, *Butler's Book,* 903–4, 907–8.
75. Louis P. Masur, "Liberty Is a Slow Fruit: Lincoln the Deliberate Emancipator," *American Scholar* 81 (Autumn 2012), 49–50.
76. "Letter from H. Ford Douglass [*sic*]," *Douglass' Monthly*, February 1863, 786.
77. Manisha Sinha, "Did He Die an Abolitionist? The Evolution of Abraham Lincoln's Antislavery," *American Political Thought* 4 (Summer 2015): 449.

78. Joseph R. Fornieri, "Lincoln on Black Citizenship," in *Constitutionalism in the Approach and Aftermath of the Civil War*, ed. Paul D. Moreno and Johnathan O'Neill (New York: Fordham University Press, 2013), 55–79.
79. Gregory T. Knouff, "White Men in Arms: Concepts of Citizenship and Masculinity in Revolutionary America," in *Representing Masculinity: Male Citizenship in Modern Western Culture*, ed. Stefan Dudink, Karen Hagemann, and Anna Clark (New York: Palgrave Macmillan, 2007), 25–40.
80. William C. Nell, *The Colored Patriots of the American Revolution* (Boston: Robert F. Wallcut, 1855); Patrick Rael, *Black Identity and Black Protest in the Antebellum North* (Chapel Hill: University of North Carolina Press, 2002), 263.
81. An Act more effectually to provide for the National Defence by establishing an Uniform Militia throughout the United States, May 8, 1792, ch. 33, *U.S. Statutes at Large* 1 (1848).
82. "Militia," ch. 70, sec. 1, in *A Compilation of the Statutes of the State of Illinois*, ed. N. H. Purple, 2 vols. (Chicago: Keen and Lee, 1856), 2:741.
83. Cain, *Lincoln's Attorney General*, 213.
84. Donald, *Inside Lincoln's Cabinet*, 96, 99–100; see also "The Employment of Negroes as Soldiers," *New York Times*, August 6, 1862, 4.
85. Lincoln, "Emancipation Proclamation," January 1, 1863, *Collected Works*, 6:28–30.
86. An Act to suppress Insurrection, to Punish Treason and Rebellion, to seize and confiscate the Property of Rebels, and for other Purposes, July 17, 1862, ch. 195, *U.S. Statutes at Large* 12 (1863), 592.
87. William C. Harris, *Lincoln and the Union Governors* (Carbondale: Southern Illinois University Press, 2013), 47–49.
88. Lincoln, "Remarks to Deputation of Western Gentlemen," August 4, 1862, *Collected Works*, 5:356–57. A letter to the *New York Times* from "A Republican" made the same argument two days later. "Arming the Negroes," *New York Times*, August 6, 1862, 2.
89. *The Diary of Orville Hickman Browning*, vol. 1, *1850–1864*, ed. Theodore Calvin Pease and James G. Randall (Springfield: Illinois State Historical Library, 1925), 555.
90. Douglass, *Life and Times*, 386–87.
91. Lincoln, "Reply to Emancipation Memorial Presented by Chicago Christians of All Denominations," September 13, 1862, *Collected Works*, 5:423.
92. Randall M. Miller and Jon W. Zophy, "Unwelcome Allies: Billy Yank and the Black Soldier," *Phylon* 39 (Third Quarter 1978): 236.
93. "The War Department. Report of Secretary Stanton," December 10, 1863, *New York Times*, 4.
94. Douglass, *Life and Times*, 376.

95. Lincoln, "Interview with Alexander W. Randall and Joseph T. Mills," *Collected Works*, 7:507.
96. James M. McPherson, *The Struggle for Equality: Abolitionists and the Negro in the Civil War and Reconstruction* (Princeton, NJ: Princeton University Press, 1964), 192–220.
97. Andrew quoted in Christian G. Samito, *Becoming American under Fire: Irish Americans, African Americans, and the Politics of Citizenship during the Civil War Era* (Ithaca, NY: Cornell University Press, 2011), 48.
98. W. E. B. Du Bois, *Black Reconstruction in America* (New York: Russell and Russell, 1935; repr., New York: Oxford University Press, 2014), 84.
99. See Laura E. Free, *Suffrage Reconstructed: Gender, Race, and Voting Rights in the Civil War Era* (Ithaca, NY: Cornell University Press, 2015), 7, 99–101; A. Kristen Foster, "'We Are Men!': Frederick Douglass and the Fault Lines of Gendered Citizenship," *Journal of the Civil War Era* 1 (June 2011): 143–75.
100. An Act to define the pay and Emoluments of Certain Officers of the Army, and for other Purposes, July 17, 1862, ch. 200, *U.S. Statutes at Large* 12 (1863), 597.
101. *Addresses of the Hon. W. D. Kelley, Miss Anna E. Dickinson, and Mr. Frederick Douglass, at a Mass Meeting, Held at National Hall, Philadelphia, July 6, 1863, for the Promotion of Colored Enlistments* (Philadelphia: n.p., 1863), 5, 7.
102. See Jim Cullen, "'I's a Man Now': Gender and African American Men," in *Divided Houses: Gender and the Civil War*, ed. Catherine Clinton and Nina Silber (New York: Oxford University Press, 1992), 76–91; John David Smith, *Lincoln and the U.S. Colored Troops* (Carbondale: Southern Illinois University Press, 2013), 113–14.
103. Faye E. Dudden, *Fighting Chance: The Struggle over Woman Suffrage and Black Suffrage in Reconstruction* (New York: Oxford University Press, 2011), 51–52, 57–59.
104. C. H. Dall, "To the Women of the Loyal League," *Liberator*, May 6, 1864, 74–75.
105. "Mrs. E. Cady Stanton to Mrs. Dall," *Liberator*, June 3, 1864, 89.
106. "The Women's National League," *New-York Daily Tribune*, May 28, 1864, 3.
107. Dudden, *Fighting Chance*, 58.
108. George Livermore, *An Historical Research Respecting the Opinions of the Founders of the Republic on Negroes as Slaves, as Citizens, and as Soldiers* (Boston: John Wilson and Son, 1862); William R. Livermore, "The Emancipation Pen," *Proceedings of the Massachusetts Historical Society* 44 (April 1911): 596.
109. Charles Sumner, "The Late George Livermore, Esq.," in *Collected Works*, 15 vols. (Boston: Lee and Shepard, 1875–1883), 9:435.

110. "Valuable Historical Research," *Liberator*, November 21, 1862, 186.
111. Livermore, *Historical Research*, 8.
112. Mark E. Neeley Jr., "The President and the Historian: Lincoln and George Livermore," *Lincoln Lore*, no. 1621 (March 1973): 3.
113. Charles Sumner to Lincoln, November 8, 1862, Abraham Lincoln Papers, Library of Congress.
114. Sumner, "Late George Livermore," 9:435.
115. Livermore, *Historical Research*, 113, 116, 118, 126, 199.
116. Lincoln to Andrew Johnson, March 26, 1863, *Collected Works*, 6:149–50.
117. Lincoln to Ulysses S. Grant, August 9, 1863, *Collected Works*, 6:374–75.
118. On Halpine and Hay, see Michael Burlingame, ed., *At Lincoln's Side: John Hay's Civil War Correspondence and Selected Writings* (Carbondale: Southern Illinois University Press, 2000), 66–71, 241–42.
119. *The Life and Adventures, Songs, Services, and Speeches of Private Miles O'Reilly* (New York: Carleton, 1864), 56.
120. "Miles O'Reilly on the 'Naygurs,'" *New York Herald*, January 17, 1864, 1.
121. See, e.g., *Cleveland Daily Leader*, January 21, 1864, 3; *Hartford Courant*, January 23, 1864, 2; *Chicago Tribune*, January 23, 1864, 3.
122. *Life and Adventures, Songs, Services, and Speeches of Private Miles O'Reilly*, 58.
123. Smith, *Lincoln and the U.S. Colored Troops*, 15–16.
124. US War Department, *The War of the Rebellion: A Compilation of the Official Records of the Union and Confederate Armies*, 128 vols. (Washington, DC: Government Printing Office, 1885), ser. 1, 14:189–91.
125. "War Department. Report of Secretary Stanton," *New York Times*, 4.
126. Ulysses S. Grant to Lincoln, August 23, 1863, Abraham Lincoln Papers, Library of Congress.
127. Lincoln to James C. Conkling, August 26, 1863, *Collected Works*, 6:406–10; "The Great Union Mass Meeting," *Daily State Journal* (Springfield, IL), September 4, 1863, 2.
128. See Dirck, *Abraham Lincoln and White America*, 131–36.
129. *Diary of Orville Hickman Browning*, 1:682–83.
130. Lincoln, "Proclamation of Amnesty and Reconstruction," December 8, 1863, *Collected Works*, 7:53–56.
131. "The Wade-Davis Bill," in *A Just and Lasting Peace: A Documentary History of Reconstruction*, ed. John David Smith (New York: Penguin Group, 2013), 18–23.
132. An Act to establish an uniform rule of Naturalization, and to repeal the acts heretofore passed on that subject, April 14, 1802, ch. 28, *U.S. Statutes at Large* 2 (1850), 153.
133. McPherson, *Battle Cry of Freedom*, 606–7.
134. An Act for enrolling and calling out the national Forces, and for other Purposes, March 3, 1863, ch. 75, *U.S. Statutes at Large* 12 (1863), 731;

Lincoln, "Proclamation concerning Aliens," May 8, 1863, *Collected Works*, 6:203–4.

135. Lincoln, "Annual Message to Congress," *Collected Works*, 7:38–39.
136. Hiroshi Motomura, *Americans in Waiting: The Lost Story of Immigration and Citizenship in the United States* (New York: Oxford University Press, 2006), 8–9.
137. An Act to Secure Homesteads to actual Settlers on the Public Domain, May 20, 1862, ch. 75, *U.S. Statutes at Large* 12 (1863), 392.
138. An Act to provide a temporary Government for the Territory of Idaho, March 3, 1863, ch. 117, *U.S. Statutes at Large* 12 (1863), 808; An Act to provide a temporary Government for the Territory of Montana, May 26, 1864, ch. 95, *U.S. Statutes at Large* 13 (1866), 87–88.
139. Lincoln, "Annual Message to Congress," December 6, 1864, *Collected Works*, 8:141.
140. An Act to define the pay and Emoluments of certain Officers of the Army, *U.S. Statutes at Large* 12, 597.
141. McPherson, *Battle Cry of Freedom*, 601.
142. An Act to amend the several Acts heretofore passed to provide for the Enrolling and Calling out the National Forces, and for other Purposes, March 3, 1865, ch. 74, *U.S. Statutes at Large* 13 (1866), 490–91.
143. Lincoln, "Proclamation Offering Pardon to Deserters," March 11, 1865, *Collected Works*, 8:349–50.
144. William A. Blair, *With Malice toward Some: Treason and Loyalty in the Civil War Era* (Chapel Hill: University of North Carolina Press, 2014), 281–86.
145. Lincoln to Henry J. Raymond, December 18, 1860, *Collected Works*, 4:156; "Lincoln an Abolitionist—the Proof from His Own Lips," *Brooklyn Daily Eagle*, October 27, 1860, 2.
146. Michael Vorenberg, "After Emancipation: Abraham Lincoln's Black Dream," in *Lincoln Revisited: New Insights from the Lincoln Forum*, ed. John Y. Simon, Harold Holzer, and Dawn Vogel (New York: Fordham University Press, 2007), 225–27.
147. Quarles, *Lincoln and the Negro*, 39–40; Hart, "Springfield's African Americans," 35–54.
148. See, e.g., John E. Washington, *They Knew Lincoln* (1942; new ed., New York: Oxford University Press, 2018), 183.
149. Douglas Walter Bristol Jr., *Knights of the Razor: Black Barbers in Slavery and Freedom* (Baltimore: Johns Hopkins University Press, 2015), 3.
150. Lincoln to Charles R. Welles, September 27, 1852, *Collected Works*, 2:159.
151. Michael Burlingame, ed., *Lincoln Observed: Civil War Dispatches of Noah Brooks* (Baltimore: Johns Hopkins University Press, 1998), 140.
152. Donald, *Lincoln*, 167; Charles N. Zucker, "The Free Negro Question: Race Relations in Ante-Bellum Illinois, 1801–1860" (PhD diss., Northwestern

University, 1972), 324–30; Mark E. Neely Jr., *The Abraham Lincoln Encyclopedia* (New York: Da Capo Press, 1982), 219; see also Natalie Sweet, "A Representative 'of our people': The Agency of William Slade, Leader in the African American Community and Usher to Abraham Lincoln," *Journal of the Abraham Lincoln Association* 34 (Summer 2013): 21–41.

153. Foner, *Fiery Trial*, 131.
154. Lincoln to Edwin M. Stanton, February 8, 1865, *Collected Works*, 8:272–73; see also Lincoln to Edwin M. Stanton, April 11, 1864, *Collected Works*, 7:295.
155. On Lincoln and Douglass see Blight, *Frederick Douglass*, 408, 436–37, 457–62; Christopher N. Breiseth, "Lincoln and Frederick Douglass: Another Debate," *Journal of the Illinois Historical Society* 68 (February 1975): 9–26; Oakes, *Radical and the Republican*; John Stauffer, *Giants: The Parallel Lives of Frederick Douglass and Abraham Lincoln* (New York: Hachette Book Group, 2008).
156. "Speech of Frederick Douglass," *Proceedings of the American Anti-Slavery Society at Its Third Decade Held in the City of Philadelphia, Dec. 3rd and 4th, 1863* (New York: American Anti-Slavery Society, 1864), 116.
157. "Fred. Douglass at Cooper Institute," *New York Herald*, January 14, 1864, 1; "Speech of Frederick Douglass," *Proceedings of the American Anti-Slavery Society*, 116.
158. "Speech of Frederick Douglass," *Proceedings of the American Anti-Slavery Society*, 117.
159. Douglass, *Life and Times*, 385–86.
160. William Shakespeare, *As You Like It*, act 2, scene 7.
161. Michael Anderegg, *Lincoln and Shakespeare* (Lawrence: University Press of Kansas, 2015), 1–51. Anderegg notes that, by the 1850s, Shakespeare's plays had become a species of cultural capital, so an allusion to Shakespeare would have lent authority to any speaker.
162. Douglass, *Life and Times*, 386.
163. Douglass, *Life and Times*, 386–87.
164. Allen Thorndike Rice, *Reminiscences of Abraham Lincoln by Distinguished Men of This Time*, 6th ed. (1886; repr., New York: North American Review, 1888), 188.
165. Douglass, *Life and Times*, 386–87.
166. Douglass, *Life and Times*, 388.
167. Douglass, *Life and Times*, 397–98; Lincoln, "Memorandum Concerning His Probable Failure of Re-election," August 23, 1864, *Collected Works*, 7:514.
168. Frederick Douglass to Lincoln, August 29, 1864, Abraham Lincoln Papers, Library of Congress.
169. Douglass, *Life and Times*, 405–7; Rice, *Reminiscences of Abraham Lincoln*, 191–93.

170. Rice, *Reminiscences of Abraham Lincoln*, 193.
171. "Dinner to Citizens of Louisiana," *Liberator*, April 15, 1864, 63.
172. Herman Belz, "Origins of Negro Suffrage during the Civil War," *Southern Studies* 17 (Summer 1978): 115–30; William C. Harris, *With Charity for All: Lincoln and the Restoration of the Union* (Lexington: University Press of Kentucky, 1997), 171–96; Lincoln to Nathaniel P. Banks, December 24, 1863, *Collected Works*, 7:89–90; "The Old Freemen of Louisiana," *Liberator*, March 11, 1864, 42.
173. "Dinner to Citizens of Louisiana," *Liberator*, 63.
174. "Petition of the Free Colored Citizens of Louisiana," *Liberator*, April 1, 1864, 55.
175. "Dinner to Citizens of Louisiana," *Liberator*, 63.
176. "Dinner to Citizens of Louisiana," *Liberator*, 63.
177. "Our Washington Letter," *Daily Ohio State Journal* (Columbus, OH), March 9, 1864, 2.
178. "From Washington," *Cleveland Daily Leader*, March 5, 1864, 1; see Harris, *With Charity for All*, 183.
179. Lincoln to Michael Hahn, March 13, 1864, *Collected Works*, 7:243.
180. Belz, "Origins of Negro Suffrage," 119.
181. Lawanda Cox, *Lincoln and Black Freedom: A Study in Presidential Leadership* (Columbia: University of South Carolina Press, 1994), 99; *Debate in the Convention for the Revision and Amendment of the Constitution of the State of Louisiana* (New Orleans: W. R. Fish, 1864), 633, 636, 638, 642.
182. David S. Cecelski, *The Fire of Freedom: Abraham Galloway and the Slaves' Civil War* (Chapel Hill: University of North Carolina Press, 2012), 115–27.
183. "Freemen of North Carolina Striking for their Rights," *Anglo-African*, May 14, 1864, 1.
184. "From Newbern," *Anglo-African*, July 2, 1864, 1.
185. "Reception of the North Carolina Delegation," *Anglo-African*, May 14, 1864, 2.
186. "From Newbern," *Anglo-African*, 1.
187. "Letter from Sojourner Truth," *National Anti-Slavery Standard*, December 17, 1864, 2.
188. Kate Masur, "Color Was a Bar to the Entrance: African American Activism and the Question of Social Equality in Lincoln's White House," *American Quarterly* 69 (March 2017): 1–22; Michael Burlingame, "African Americans at White House Receptions during Lincoln's Administration. Part I," *Journal of the Abraham Lincoln Association* 41 (Summer 2020): 47–64; William O. Stoddard, *Inside the White House in War Times: Memoirs and Reports of Lincoln's Secretary*, ed. Michael Burlingame (Lincoln: University of Nebraska Press, 2000), 172.

189. Power-Greene, *Against Wind and Tide*, 2–3.
190. Power-Greene, *Against Wind and Tide*, 60–61.
191. Lincoln, "Last Public Address," April 11, 1865, *Collected Works*, 8:403; Louis P. Masur, *Lincoln's Last Speech: Wartime Reconstruction and the Crisis of Reunion* (New York: Oxford University Press, 2015).
192. Edward D. Neill, *Reminiscences of the Last Year of President Lincoln's Life* (St. Paul, MN: Pioneer Press, 1885), 16.
193. Lincoln, "Address on Colonization," *Collected Works*, 5: 372–73.
194. Anbinder, *Nativism and Slavery*, 138, 248, 254; Keyssar, *Right to Vote*, 53, 67, 69.
195. Herman Belz, *Reconstructing the Union: Theory and Policy during the Civil War* (Ithaca, NY: Cornell University Press, 1969), 260–61.
196. Ari Berman, *Give Us the Ballot: The Modern Struggle for Voting Rights in America* (New York: Farrar, Strauss, and Giroux, 2015), 17, 32–34; Allan J. Lichtman, *The Embattled Vote in America: From the Founding to the Present* (Cambridge, MA: Harvard University Press, 2018), 94–95, 139–40.
197. John W. Blassingame, *The Slave Community: Plantation Life in the Antebellum South*, rev. ed. (New York: Oxford University Press, 1979), 312.
198. Eric Foner, *Reconstruction: America's Unfinished Revolution, 1863–1877* (New York: Harper and Row, 1988), 74.
199. Lincoln, "Proclamation of Amnesty and Reconstruction," December 8, 1863, *Collected Works*, 7:53–56.
200. Xi Wang, *The Trial of Democracy: Black Suffrage and Northern Republicans, 1860–1910* (Athens: University of Georgia Press, 1997), 7–18.
201. An Act to provide a temporary Government for the Territory of Idaho, ch. 117, March 3, 1863, *U.S. Statutes at Large* 12 (1863), 810.
202. An Act to provide a temporary Government for the Territory of Montana, ch. 95, May 26, 1864, *U.S. Statutes at Large* 13 (1866), 87–88.
203. Belz, "Origins of Negro Suffrage during the Civil War," 124.
204. Burlingame and Ettlinger, *Inside Lincoln's White House*, 253, 368n319.
205. John C. Rodrigue, *Lincoln and Reconstruction* (Carbondale: Southern Illinois University Press, 2013), 121–22.
206. Wade-Davis Bill, February 15, 1864, in *A Just and Lasting Peace: A Documentary History of Reconstruction*, ed. John David Smith (New York: Penguin Group, 2013), 22.
207. Burlingame, *Abraham Lincoln*, 2:803.

Conclusion: "The Great Task Remaining"

1. An Act to protect all Persons in the United States, and furnish the Means of their Vindication, April 9, 1866, ch. 31, *U. S. Statutes at Large* 14 (1868), 27.
2. Foner, *Second Founding*.

3. "Speech of Wendell Phillips, Esq.," *National Anti-Slavery Standard*, May 13, 1865, 2.
4. Frederick Douglass, Eulogy on Abraham Lincoln, June 1, 1865, Frederick Douglass Papers, Library of Congress.
5. W. E. B. Du Bois, "The World and Us," *Crisis*, July 1922, 103.
6. Lincoln, "Address Delivered at the Dedication of the Cemetery at Gettysburg," November 19, 1863, *Collected Works*, 7:19; Berman, *Give Us the Ballot*; Lichtman, *Embattled Vote in America*.

SELECT BIBLIOGRAPHY

Anbinder, Tyler. *Nativism and Slavery: The Northern Know Nothings and the Politics of the 1850s.* New York: Oxford University Press, 1994.

Belz, Herman. "Origins of Negro Suffrage during the Civil War." *Southern Studies* 17 (Summer 1978): 115–30.

Blight, David W. *Frederick Douglass: Prophet of Freedom.* New York: Simon and Schuster, 2018.

Burlingame, Michael. *Abraham Lincoln: A Life.* 2 vols. Baltimore: Johns Hopkins University Press, 2008.

Cain, Marvin R. *Lincoln's Attorney General: Edward Bates of Missouri.* Columbia: University of Missouri Press, 1965.

Davis, Rodney O., and Douglas L. Wilson, eds. *The Lincoln-Douglas Debates.* Urbana: University of Illinois Press, 2008.

Dirck, Brian. *Abraham Lincoln and White America.* Lawrence: University Press of Kansas, 2012.

Donald, David. *Lincoln.* New York: Simon and Schuster, 1995.

Fehrenbacher, Don E. *The* Dred Scott *Case: Its Significance in American Law and Politics.* New York: Oxford University Press, 1978.

Foner, Eric. *The Fiery Trial: Abraham Lincoln and American Slavery.* New York: W. W. Norton, 2010.

———. *Free Soil, Free Labor, Free Men: The Ideology of the Republican Party before the Civil War.* 1970. Reprint, New York: Oxford University Press, 1995.

Fornieri, Joseph R. "Lincoln on Black Citizenship." In *Constitutionalism in the Approach and Aftermath of the Civil War,* edited by Paul D. Moreno and Johnathan O'Neill, 55–79. New York: Fordham University Press, 2013.

Guyatt, Nicholas. *Bind Us Apart: How Enlightened Americans Invented Racial Segregation.* New York: Basic Books, 2016.

Harris, William C. *With Charity for All: Lincoln and the Restoration of the Union.* Lexington: University Press of Kentucky, 1997.

Hart, Richard E. "Springfield's African Americans as a Part of the Lincoln Community." *Journal of the Abraham Lincoln Association* 20 (Winter 1999): 35–54.

Holt, Michael F. *The Rise and Fall of the American Whig Party: Jacksonian Politics and the Onset of the Civil War.* New York: Oxford University Press, 1999.

Kettner, James H. *The Development of American Citizenship, 1608–1870.* Chapel Hill: University of North Carolina Press, 1978.

Keyssar, Alexander. *The Right to Vote: The Contested History of Democracy in the United States.* Rev. ed. New York: Basic Books, 2009.

Levine, Bruce. "'The Vital Element of the Republican Party': Antislavery, Nativism, and Abraham Lincoln." *Journal of the Civil War Era* 1 (December 2011): 481–505.

Litwack, Leon F. *North of Slavery: The Negro in the Free States, 1790–1860.* Chicago: University of Chicago Press, 1961.

Magness, Phillip W., and Sebastian N. Page. *Colonization after Emancipation: Lincoln and the Movement for Black Resettlement.* Columbia: University of Missouri Press, 2011.

Masur, Kate. "The African American Delegation to Abraham Lincoln: A Reappraisal." *Civil War History* 56 (June 2010): 117–44.

McPherson, James M. *Battle Cry of Freedom: The Civil War Era.* New York: Oxford University Press, 1988.

Miller, Richard Lawrence. *Lincoln and His World: Prairie Politician 1834–1842.* Mechanicsburg, PA: Stackpole Books, 2008.

Neely, Mark E., Jr. "Colonization and the Myth That Lincoln Prepared the People for Emancipation." In *Lincoln's Proclamation: Emancipation Reconsidered*, edited by William A. Blair and Karen Fisher Younger, 45–74. Chapel Hill: University of North Carolina Press, 2009.

Oakes, James. *Freedom National: The Destruction of Slavery in the United States, 1861–1865.* New York: W. W. Norton, 2013.

———. *The Radical and the Republican: Frederick Douglass, Abraham Lincoln, and the Triumph of Antislavery Politics.* New York: W. W. Norton, 2007.

Paludan, Phillip Shaw. "Lincoln and Colonization: Policy or Propaganda?" *Journal of the Abraham Lincoln Association* 25 (Winter 2004): 23–37.

Power-Greene, Ousmane K. *Against Wind and Tide: The African American Struggle against the Colonization Movement.* New York: New York University Press, 2014.

Quarles, Benjamin. *Lincoln and the Negro.* New York: Oxford University Press, 1962.

Silverman, Jason H. *Lincoln and the Immigrant.* Carbondale: Southern Illinois University Press, 2015.

Smith, John David. *Lincoln and the U.S. Colored Troops.* Carbondale: Southern Illinois University Press, 2013.

Tomek, Beverly C., and Matthew J. Hetrick, eds. *New Directions in the Study of African American Recolonization.* Gainesville: University Press of Florida, 2017.

Voegeli, V. Jacque. *Free but Not Equal: The Midwest and the Negro during the Civil War.* Chicago: University of Chicago Press, 1967.

Vorenberg, Michael. "Abraham Lincoln and the Politics of Black Colonization." *Journal of the Abraham Lincoln Association* 14 (Summer 1993): 23–45.

———. "Abraham Lincoln's 'Fellow Citizens'—before and after Emancipation." In *Lincoln's Proclamation: Emancipation Reconsidered*, edited by William A. Blair and Karen Fisher Younger, 151–69. Chapel Hill: University of North Carolina Press, 2009.

Wilentz, Sean. *The Rise of American Democracy: Jefferson to Lincoln.* New York: W. W. Norton, 2005.

Williamson, Chilton. *American Suffrage: From Property to Democracy, 1760–1860.* Princeton, NJ: Princeton University Press, 1960.

Wilson, Douglas L. *Honor's Voice: The Transformation of Abraham Lincoln.* New York: Alfred A. Knopf, 1998.

Wilson, Douglas L., and Rodney O. Davis, eds. *Herndon's Informants: Letters, Interviews, and Statements about Abraham Lincoln.* Urbana: University of Illinois Press, 1998.

Winkle, Kenneth J. *The Young Eagle: The Rise of Abraham Lincoln.* Dallas: Taylor Trade Publishing, 2001.

INDEX

Page numbers in italics indicate illustrations.

Mark E. Steiner, a professor of law and associate dean at South Texas College of Law Houston, is the author of *An Honest Calling: The Law Practice of Abraham Lincoln*. Steiner received both his law degree and a doctorate in history from the University of Houston. He twice has been awarded Fulbright scholarships and is actively involved in pro bono efforts to assist immigrants on the path toward citizenship.

This series of concise books fills a need for short studies of the life, times, and legacy of President Abraham Lincoln. Each book gives readers the opportunity to quickly achieve basic knowledge of a Lincoln-related topic. These books bring fresh perspectives to well-known topics, investigate previously overlooked subjects, and explore in greater depth topics that have not yet received book-length treatment. For a complete list of current and forthcoming titles, see www.conciselincolnlibrary.com.

Other Books in the Concise Lincoln Library

Abraham Lincoln and Horace Greeley
Gregory A. Borchard

Lincoln and the Civil War
Michael Burlingame

Lincoln's Sense of Humor
Richard Carwardine

Lincoln and the Constitution
Brian R. Dirck

Lincoln in Indiana
Brian R. Dirck

Lincoln and Native Americans
Michael S. Green

Lincoln and the Election of 1860
Michael S. Green

Lincoln and Congress
William C. Harris

Lincoln and the Union Governors
William C. Harris

Lincoln and the Abolitionists
Stanley Harrold

Lincoln's Campaign Biographies
Thomas A. Horrocks

Lincoln in the Illinois Legislature
Ron J. Keller

Lincoln and the Military
John F. Marszalek

Lincoln and Emancipation
Edna Greene Medford

Lincoln and the American Founding
Lucas E. Morel

Lincoln and Reconstruction
John C. Rodrigue

Lincoln and the Thirteenth Amendment
Christian G. Samito

Lincoln and Medicine
Glenna R. Schroeder-Lein

Lincoln and the Immigrant
Jason H. Silverman

Lincoln and the U.S. Colored Troops
John David Smith

Lincoln's Assassination
Edward Steers, Jr.

Lincoln and Race
Richard Striner

Lincoln and Religion
Ferenc Morton Szasz with Margaret Connell Szasz

Lincoln and the Natural Environment
James Tackach

Lincoln and the War's End
John C. Waugh

Lincoln as Hero
Frank J. Williams

Abraham and Mary Lincoln
Kenneth J. Winkle